Adventure Sports

ADVANCED
SKIING

Adventure Sports

ADVANCED
SKIING

MARTYN HURN

STACKPOLE
BOOKS

Cameron and Kelker Streets • P.O. Box 1831 • Harrisburg, PA 17105

A STACKPOLE BOOK

First published in Great Britain by
Salamander Books Limited,
London 1990
© Salamander Books Ltd

ISBN 0-8117-3027-1

Published by Stackpole Books
Cameron and Kelker Streets
PO Box 1831
Harrisburg, PA 17105

Edited by: Mark Bathurst
Designed by: Rod Ferring

Typeset by: Flairplan Ltd
Artwork by: Denise Nicholls
Color reproductions by: Magnum
Graphics Ltd
Printed in Belgium

The author
Martyn Hurn is a qualified ski coach, a member of the British Association of Ski Instructors and a qualified mountaineering instructor. He has climbed and skied worldwide, including as far afield as North Africa and the Himalayas. He favours a holistic approach to coaching, believing that the needs of the mind and body must be balanced if a skier's full potential is to be realised. His method is further informed by experience gained working with other instructors, both American and European. Martyn has had two skiing books published previously, *Skiing Real Snow* and *Monoskiing*. His instructional style is straightforward and clear, and his writing, which is punctuated with personal anecdotes drawn from his wide experience, reflects this clarity and his tremendous enthusiasm for this great sport.

The illustrator
Denise Nicholls is a freelance illustrator and designer based in Aberystwyth, Wales. A technical illustrator by training, she has worked on a variety of books, including both of Martyn Hurn's previous titles. She has a degree in Environmental Biology and enjoys travel and outdoor pursuits, especially mountaineering.

ACKNOWLEDGEMENTS
'Could you do that once more? I need the shots for the book!' Those words have nearly ostracised me from my skiing friends but to Alex Leaf, Michelle Fuller and Fred Foxon, who have heard them more than most, I must offer my special thanks. I hope they now think their patience and perseverance worth-while.

When the snow missed the Alps yet again we flew to the Summit Counties of Colorado (thanks to Salamander Books) to shoot the photographs. There we met some of the friendliest skiers in what must be some of the friendliest ski resorts in the world. Special thanks must go to John McEwan and Tom Newman of the Keystone Ski School, to Barb Keller at Keystone, to Rachel Flood at Copper Mountain, to Jim Felton at Breckenridge, to the resort of Vail and to Jupitor Jones of the Steamboat Powder Cats.

Back home I am again thankful to Denise Nicholls for her ability to turn my garbled explanations into clear, precise diagrams.

Many ski coaches have been influential in shaping my thinking but here I would like to single out Hamish Webb, Alex Leaf, John Mason and Fred Foxon. As for those on whom I have tested my ideas, I am indebted to the 'Real Snow' team of Squalor Tours, who for the last four years have suffered under my tutelage. Thank you Tony, Roger, Bevis, Rick, Rupert, John, Scirard, Paul and Pete.

Phoenix, Look, Nordica and Dynastar have yet again kept me going with superb kit, for which I thank them.

Finally, to all my long-suffering friends who for the last six months have been greeted by 'Sorry, I've got to work on the book' – I haven't any more. It's finished and I'm dying for a beer!

Martyn Hurn
February 1990

CONTENTS

INTRODUCTION

This book has been written specifically for the recreational skier. It is not for the racer or the potential instructor, but for the skier who feels that his or her parallel turns are not all they might be. You may be stemming slightly, or perhaps your edges keep washing out. You may be restricted to only a few ways of turning or want to explore new areas of skiing, such as the bumps or the powder. It is for the skier who wants the maximum enjoyment out of the sport.

Advanced skiing is many things to many people. Who are the best skiers? Are they the Giradellis and Klammers of the race world? Are they the extreme skiers, the Jean Marc Boivins and Glen Plakes, or are they perhaps the old alpine Guides who seem able to cruise down through the very worst snow that nature throws at them? Many years ago I watched a film about Jean Claude Killy, one of the greatest racers of his day, skiing with a group of freestylers who were also at the tops of their disciplines. The film started with each testing the others on their home ground, but then they moved to the open mountain, to the bumps and to the powder. Suddenly no one was the best, they were all as good as each other. Each had a distinctive, recognisable style but they all skied superbly, and I had found my ski model. It wasn't a particular individual that struck me but the group's versatility, each skier's ability to ski anything well, the only common factor being the way in which they were able to work their skis.

The skill to ski this way comes from a solid foundation of ski technique and many miles of skiing. If the fundamentals of your skiing are sound, you can develop your own personal style in whatever direction you wish. I dread the day when the slopes are full of clones of the ski schools' latest style. We should all be recognisable as ourselves, especially as advanced skiers. The only common elements should be that we are able, because of the sound base of our technique, to ski according to the mood of the day and that we are having fun. Bear this in mind and start by drawing from the book those things that strike a chord with you. The skills dealt with are not presented in any linear sequence (with the exception of one section in 'Cruising with Style'), so it is possible to dip into the text and work on those that appeal most.

You will find several themes running through the book. The first is the importance I attach to versatility, because my own ski model is still the versatile skier. The second is recognition that our skiing moods vary. Some days you will want to ski calmly, others to take your excitement threshold to its limits; some days to concentrate on technical excellence, others to throw efficiency to the wind and enjoy the extremes of athletic movement. The third is my reliance on you to experiment within the frameworks I offer, to convert my words into feelings and images and to get out onto the slope and try out my suggestions. That way your skiing will take a step forward and your efforts on the slope, and mine in writing this book, will be rewarded. At this level of skiing I favour a holistic approach, both in the way I present techniques and in the sense that I do not break techniques down into exercises. I prefer you to try them by skiing the mountain, linking one turn to the next. Some of the turns function as exercises, but because I have treated them as turns in their own right they, and the learning process, become more enjoyable.

At the start of each section I describe the terrain most suitable for learning the technique in question. Using terrain to the greatest advantage is one of the most important skills of the advanced skier; it will come only with miles and miles of constructive practice. For this reason I recommend that you choose your own line down the mountainside, noticing how the nuances of slope variation affect your performance. This is especially relevant to those of you who have spent many years under the tutelage of instructors.

Finally, remember that skiing, advanced or otherwise, is about having fun, not just technique. Many potential advanced skiers get hung up on the technicalities of the sport. Skiing can be enjoyed on many levels and that of technical excellence is certainly one of them, but there are plenty of others. I hope the following pages help you to appreciate some of them.

Martyn Hurn.

CHAPTER 1

FUN IN THE SUN

It had been a good day – some great bumps runs and a small amount of powder. We were both skiing well. It was decided to go higher up the mountain, but as soon as we got on the chairlift the cloud came down. When we dismounted we could hardly see the start of the run. It was a total whiteout.

Above: It was horrendous, but there he was, cruising along . . .

I had not gone more than 50 metres before I was on my backside. I picked myself up and tried again; this time it only took two turns before I was over. It was horrendous. I could feel myself getting tenser and tenser. My shoulders were tight and my legs were like planks of wood. I was skiing worse with every turn, and every time I managed to look up there he was, cruising along as though there was nothing unusual about the conditions. Normally we skied to the same standard. At least he could appear to be struggling – after all, we were supposed to be friends!

Things didn't get any better and finally I could stand it no more. He was still cruising along and I was still falling over.

'So what's the secret?' I cried out in frustration. 'How is it I'm falling all over the place and you're skiing as though nothing was different?'

'What, me?' he replied, as though the whole mountainside was covered in people dancing along merrily on their skis. 'I just imagine I'm still having fun in the sun.'

His rather glib reply did nothing for my confidence, and a very strained descent followed, at least for me.

It was a long time before I realised that he had probably been closer to the truth than I had thought. He literally had been imagining himself skiing in the sun, and this had helped him to relax in the otherwise difficult conditions. The influence of our minds over our ability to perform is very powerful and, I am sure, will be recognised to some degree by all of you. This incident graphically illustrates how a friend used a simple mental technique to help himself relax and cope under adverse circumstances. Mental techniques, however, are not the secret of easy success. They

require as much effort and commitment as physical techniques, but equally you may, with perseverance, discover some that will transform your skiing. Advanced skiing demands a balance between being able to perform techniques well, having the right amount of experience and being in the right frame of mind to be able to apply techniques skilfully. Without the physical techniques you will not ski well, but equally if your mental attitude is not right, you will also have no success. They are of equal importance. Many of the blocks to learning are mental rather than physical, and creating a positive learning environment is as much to do with the mind as it is to do with the body and the terrain.

The reason I am starting with this topic is that in order to get the most out of the technical explanations I am going to present, it is important that you understand how best to

Below: Having fun in the sun.

exploit your learning potential. I believe you will learn at this level only by experimenting. My role is to offer guidelines which will lead you in the right direction but within them you must experiment so as to find out what works for you. There can be no absolutes because there are so many variables. Take the action of edging your skis as an example. The amount you need to edge them is dependent on your body type, your skis, your speed, where you want to go, the state of the snow, etc. I have likened this situation in the past to learning to drive a car. Your instructor does not tell you to push the brake pedal down a specified amount in order to stop at a junction; you quickly learn how hard to press by experimenting. Before long you are able to stop perfectly and all your instructor has done is tell you to brake, perhaps adding 'harder' in the early stages. Fortunately the consequences of

edging too little are rarely as serious as those of braking late!

Advanced skiing is all about dynamic balance, our ability to balance over our skis on a variety of terrains and in a variety of situations. This balance can only be developed through constructive miles of skiing, and making these miles as constructive as possible is, first, about being in a receptive frame of mind and, second, about experimenting with different techniques.

How can we make the most of these factors? We all tend to have a favoured system for absorbing information. Some people respond well to visual stimuli, others to auditory and others to physical. If you think back to your earlier ski classes, you may remember how some people always preferred to watch the instructor, others needed a precise description and some just needed to get on with it so they could feel what was happening.

Good instructors take this into account and present a technique in a number of guises in the hope that one strikes a chord with you. I have written this book ever mindful of these various learning strategies. The diagrams and photo sequences are exact, the descriptions are concise and the sensations you should be searching for are explained. Though you may think you know which strategy you normally adopt, it is always best to consider all of them as there is usually a degree of overlap and the bias may change from day to day. Furthermore, the more comprehensive your ability to absorb and interpret information, the more you will heighten your awareness, which in turn will enhance your enjoyment as well as your ability to perform.

Below: Dynamic balance is the key to advanced skiing.

MENTAL REHEARSAL

Let us start examining these ideas by considering the incident I related to you at the beginning of the chapter. My friend used a technique known as imaging, one of a number of so-called mental rehearsal techniques. Most of these are for use before an event, although as we have seen it is occasionally possible to use them as you are performing. These techniques are also referred to collectively by the term 'visualisation', which is a bit of a misnomer because it suggests something entirely visual, which as we shall see is not strictly the case.

To gain the most from these techniques you need to practise them in a relaxed but alert state of mind. I find the best way to reach this state is by controlling my breathing. Sitting myself in a comfortable chair or lying down, I focus my attention on my breathing. You may be able to do just that as you read these words. Notice whether you are breathing through your nose or your mouth; sense the way in which your chest is moving; are you using your diaphragm and how long is each breath? When you are totally aware of your breathing cycle, notice how the muscles in your neck and shoulders feel. Relax them if they have remained tense. Move down the rest of your body in the same way.

You should now be relaxed and yet you will be aware of small noises around you. Without moving your head or your eyes you will be aware of objects on the periphery of your vision, and this is what I mean by being relaxed and yet alert. With practice you will find that this state can be enhanced.

Now you are in this state I want you to picture in your mind's eye a good skier coming down the slope towards you. There is another skier behind, and you notice the chairlift up to your right – you can hear the clank as the chairs pass the pylon. You can also see the trees to your left. Now begin to focus on the skier and eliminate the other parts of the picture until all you are aware of is the skier (who is of the same sex as yourself). Notice the smoothness

and rhythm of the skier's turns. Sense that rhythm in your own body. Let your body sway to the same rhythm and feel the muscles in your legs tense and relax according to whether you are turning to the right or to the left. Pole plant as the skier pole plants. Feel the pressure under your feet. Hear the slight scrape of the edges of the skis against the snow. It is you who is now skiing down the slope. Slowly build up the picture again. Hear the chairlift above and behind you. The trees are to your right and you can hear another skier behind you. Feel the cold air on your face, especially as you speed up around your turns . . . The more realistic you make the scenario the more effective the rehearsal will be, so be sure to employ all of your senses. Although you may not be moving very much as you sit or lie there, your muscles and nerves will actually be responding and will be 'learning' their job so that when you actually put the manoeuvre into practice, the pathways will already be partly open.

This exercise can be done at home or just before a run on the slope. It is also possible to run it like a slow-motion movie, which can help you to focus on a particular feature of a movement sequence. There will be occasions when it is good to replace the skier with someone to whose skiing you aspire. It could be an instructor, a friend or even a famous racer,

though I find it is most effective if it is a skier whose level of ability is actually attainable. You do not necessarily need to have seen that person perform in this particular situation – you know they would cope with it and that is enough. Similarly it can also be useful to imagine yourself skiing a run which you would not normally attempt.

This is a form of imaging; that is, you are creating in your mind a situation that does not exist in actual fact, just as my friend did in the whiteout. You can use this in many ways; for example, picturing something that is synonymous with the sensation you are seeking, such as a bird swooping if you are trying to swoop around your turns. If in your imagination you fall, accept it and try to analyse why you fell. Then get up, return to the top and repeat the run without falling, making sure you do not repeat the mistakes of your previous attempt.

The variations of how to use the techniques of mental rehearsal are limitless and you can easily devise your own, but remember that what you are creating in your mind's eye should be attainable. It should be positive and it should involve as many of the senses as possible unless you are specifically trying to focus on one in particular.

Below: If you are skiing with good skiers, use them as models for mental rehearsal.

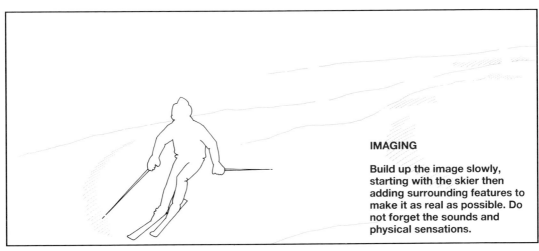

IMAGING

Build up the image slowly, starting with the skier then adding surrounding features to make it as real as possible. Do not forget the sounds and physical sensations.

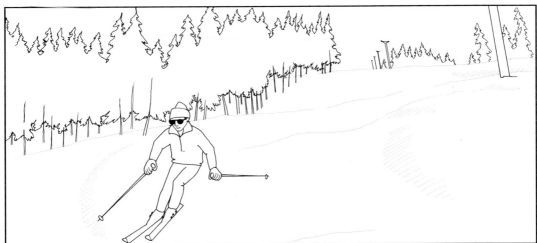

CONCENTRATION

Often when we make mistakes it is because there has been a lapse in our concentration or our concentration has been diverted onto the wrong thing. No one skis at 100 per cent all the time, but it is important not to allow these odd errors to interrupt your skiing. The exercises I have just described can help you to zero in on the most important aspects of what you are trying to achieve, but there are also a number of other techniques that can help.

At the beginning of this chapter I spoke of the different ways in which we tend to absorb information. Many people favour a verbal–auditory strategy. This is the case for many adults, yet it can be inhibiting because if you are inundated with technical information, you are not able to concentrate on the most important features. To pinch a phrase from another ski author, 'Analysis leads to paralysis.' It is for this reason that I have kept many of my technical explanations extremely simple. By so doing I do not mean to be condescending about your ability to understand exactly what is taking place – I just do not believe that any further information would be of any benefit. After all, this book is written for the recreational skier, not the ski instructor who does need to understand technique in minute detail.

The use of single words that both remind you of and reflect the movement can be very beneficial. Words can even be replaced by simple sounds and help not only with the action required but also with its timing. They help you to concentrate on what it is you are trying to do, but they must be the right words and they must be said in the right way. Take a simple jump as an example. Say 'Jump' as you leap straight up into the air. If you say the word without any energy, your jump will also be lifeless, whereas if you shout it, your jump will have spring in it. Some words are best said with an inhalation of breath, others with an exhalation. Make sure your choice suits your breathing pattern.

Concentration is vital but does not entail the tight, tense condition many will associate with the concept. It is the relaxed state of being aware of all that is around you and at the same time being able to filter out that which is of no use to you. When you lose it, concentrate on breathing control. This is best approached through the exhalation phase. Alternatively use words as I have described above, or visualise what it is you are trying to do. With practice you will find which techniques help you best.

Often your concentration will be broken by invading negative thoughts, usually initiated by fear. For example, you have been skiing a run well and suddenly you come around a bend and are faced by a steep bump field. You stop to catch your breath and then doubt creeps in. 'How do I get down this. I can't ski bumps very well. It's so long . . .' We have all been there, I

Top left: Notice the concentration on the racer's face.

Bottom left: Concentration and breathing control.

Below: Break up a daunting slope into a number of attainable goals.

am sure. When I am faced with such a situation, I use a technique which I call the North Face technique. I have done a lot of mountaineering and often when I approach a big climb such as a big North Face route, I am totally in awe of it. I stand there thinking 'No way', yet if I look more closely, I begin to see that I can climb that crack system up to there, and then up that snow-field, yes, I can cope with that; then there is a gulley that looks okay, and so on. Before I know it I can see a way up by dividing the climb into a number of attainable goals. I tackle the bump slope in just the same way, dividing it into attainable goals.

Goal setting

Goal setting is not only useful in this context but should be an integral part of your learning strategy. Appropriate goal setting reduces periods of doubt and negative thoughts to a minimum and, if done correctly, also helps to prevent the plateaux of learning that I am sure you have already experienced. The goals that you set yourself can be long term – for example, skiing a particularly difficult bump field by the end of a week's holiday – or, as in the North Face technique, short term – 'I want to get down the next

50 metres of this slope.' In either case it is important that your goals are realistic, and even then there is a risk of both mental blocks and anxiety. Mental blocks occur when you have attained your goal but have not prepared for that moment, resulting in a plateau in your learning curve. Prepare for this moment with some imaging exercises which present you skiing beyond your immediate goal. Also, as you feel you are getting close to achieving your objective, have in mind your next goal. Anxiety occurs if you feel you are not going to reach your goal and can be the result of setting your goal too high or, simply, of outright failure. I cope with both of these by reminding myself that skiing is basically fun and that I can enjoy it at many levels. I do get satisfaction in performing well but at the end of the day it is just sliding around on skis in the mountains that is most important to me. This gives me a let-out when things go wrong, and the negative experience of not attaining my goals is outweighed by the pleasure I feel at being able still to enjoy the true essence of my skiing. I can then return with a fresh set of goals that are more appropriate and that enhance my enjoyment. Consequently I find I ski in a more relaxed fashion once again.

RELAXATION

'Try to relax more' is almost as frequent a cry from the ski instructor as 'Bend ze knees', but how do you? It is one of those things that is easy to say but often very difficult to do. You may not even be aware that you are tense, yet it is vital to be relaxed in order to ski well. By this I do not mean relaxed to the point of nearly falling asleep, rather in a state of being in which your mind is alert and your body is able to tense only those muscles that are necessary to perform the manoeuvre in question. You can almost turn this argument around and talk in terms of being correctly aroused. The adrenalin is running but only sufficiently to cope with the situation; any more or less would result in a poor performance. Mental rehearsal is an excellent way of 'psyching' yourself up, but how do you reverse the process if you have overdone it. The perceptive observer will notice that you are tense through a variety of small body signs and may even pick up on slight changes in the way you act and in what you say. This provides us with the first clue. Give yourself a total body scan and isolate those areas where the tension is occurring. This process in itself may relax you. Most of us actually have a 'key', a part of the body which, if relaxed, helps to relax the rest of the body. For me it is my shoulders. At the start of a run I always give them a shake to make sure they are feeling loose and I often repeat this shake during the first few turns. The total body scan approach should eventually help you to isolate your key and then you will be able to use it whenever you think you are tense and even, as I do, at the start of a run.

This technique is really one of fine tuning and there are times when it is inadequate. On these occasions you must look outside of yourself and try to isolate the factors that are making you so tight. Fear and apprehension are the usual culprits but other factors, such as excessive peer group pressure or just plain fatigue, can play a significant role. Once you have isolated the problem there are a number of ploys that you can engage to help. Let us start by tackling fear.

The concept of control

Fear usually raises its ugly head when you no longer feel in control of a situation. The concept of control is an important one in advanced skiing. Consider for a moment the mogul masters, those bump skiers *par excellence*. When you watch them, not only are you impressed by the speed and directness with which they approach the bumps, but also by the fact that they seem to be in control. Yet ask yourself if they could actually stop quickly and the answer is, of course, no. So are they in control? In a sense yes and in another sense no. They are in control because they know that although they cannot stop immediately they can ski down to the bottom and stop there. When you were a beginner you were probably very conscious of the fact that you could not stop immediately, and this is what control meant to you then. Yet as you got better you learnt that you could turn to miss obstacles and also that, although you could not actually stop on that spot, you could stop within a few metres and that was fine. As you progressed, so the distance over which you could stop extended and your concept of control expanded. But at each hurdle in your development it

will still be one of the stumbling blocks, therefore you should develop a strategy for overcoming it each time. If I am in the mood for really blasting through the bumps and know that my level of control will be stretched to the maximum, I can never start unless the slope is really clear of other skiers. This is not only out of a sense of respect for the safety of others, but also because it allows me to expand my own concept of control in a relatively safe environment. When I return to my normal speed, I find that I appear to be so much more aware and to have more time. Skiing fast is not only exhilarating but also makes me more confident at slower speeds – provided, that is, I have chosen my moments to go fast appropriately.

We should examine this idea of control a little further because I imagine that for most of you control means keeping your speed down, yet there will come a stage when control will also mean building your speed up or at least maintaining it. This leads to another notion – that of whether you ski offensively or defensively.

First, let me say that skiing offensively does not mean aggressively and is not a macho notion. It is

Below: Expand your concept of control. Do you think this skier is in control?

about being in control in the truest sense and not allowing the situation to take over. The very best skiers ski almost totally offensively, whereas most of us have a level at which we turn to defensive skiing. In an ideal world one would learn to ski offensively and move up gradually through more and more difficult terrain with offensive techniques. The reality, however, is that many skiers do not have the time or the commitment to pursue this path, and we all like to try difficult runs even if we have to ski them defensively. However, I am not going to let you off that easily because I do want to encourage you in the offensive direction even though I have included techniques from defensive skiing in the book. Nevertheless, we all have a stop point, beyond which we prefer to ski defensively, and that is good. Without it all the north faces in the Alps would become bump fields! Finally, let me emphasise that skiing defensively on slopes that take you near the limit of your capabilities is not, and should never become, a negative experience. Defensive skiing can be smooth, rhythmical, very satisfying, and enjoyable.

CONFIDENCE

Confident skiing comes not only from a solid grounding in techniques but from miles of constructive skiing, from being comfortable with your self image and from being adequately prepared. The first factor is dealt with in the middle chapters of the book; I cannot help you directly with the second, but I can suggest ways in which the third and fourth may be improved.

Self image
Self image is a strange phenomenon in that it is forever changing and is influenced by factors that we often prefer to deny. But because it is a *self* image – in other words, created by ourselves – we can also change it. The first task is to become more aware of how we see ourselves, then we can tackle the negative aspects. Many of you will be quite happy with what you find but for the majority of us there is usually something that provokes a negative reaction. I am forever grateful to my mother who, when as a child I said, 'I can't do that', would always reply that there was no such word as *can't*. At first I thought she

Above: When a slope is crowded, it is harder to concentrate.

was talking literally, but as I matured I realised the true philosophy behind her statement. Turning negative reactions into positive ones is a slow process that must become part of your whole make-up and be reinforced by the tackling of the root causes behind them. Imagine, for example, that you find yourself saying, 'I can't ski this slope, it's too steep.' It isn't enough just to turn the phrase around and say, 'I can ski this slope even though it is steep.' You must also tackle the problem of steep slopes by, for example, finding a steep but short slope where the consequences of a slip would cause no harm, playing around on it until you are happy there, then moving on to a slightly longer one, all the time reminding yourself that, 'Yes, I am happy on this. I *can* cope with this slope.' It can be a slow transformation but with perseverance and determination you will be able to tackle all your negative attitudes. Each hurdle you cross will help you to improve your self image.

PREPARATION

Advanced skiing not only puts more demands on your mind, but also, of course, on your body and your equipment. It is important that you are confident that your equipment is not only up to the task ahead, but also that it is in good condition. A similar argument should be applied to your body. Let me deal first with equipment.

Clothing

Clothing has two functions. It protects us from the elements and it is a form of statement about ourselves. There are those who enjoy wearing the latest in fashion and those who actually prefer to dress down. Which ever camp you are in, and there are many others between these two extremes, the only thing that is important is that you feel comfortable in your clothing. Not just physically comfortable, but also mentally comfortable.

At this stage of your skiing career I am sure you have a good idea about what you like wearing, but let me make a few points relating to the demands on the advanced skier.

As you push yourself harder and harder so the demands on your body will increase. It is therefore essential that you keep it as warm as is comfortable, as this will help to prevent injury and allow it to perform more fluidly and quickly.

Your improvements in technique may allow you to ski terrain that hitherto has not been open to you, and this may make new demands upon you. Skiing away from the prepared slopes is a classic example. It is essential that your clothing can respond to the stresses this environment may put upon it. High-fashion suits are not always made of high-performance fabrics and their design may be found wanting when conditions are bad. Two-piece suits are versatile, but one-piece suits are usually warmer. On some of the longer routes it may not be possible to ski quickly back to a hut or restaurant as the weather turns bad and you will have to cope with what you are carrying. Jackets and trousers should remain warm and dry even in the worst conditions. Whatever system you use it must be adaptable, because storms can arrive quickly and if you are caught a long way from the

runs, you could be in trouble. Your jacket should have a light wind-proof hood that can be stored away when it is not needed. I supplement this and my normal ski hat with a motorcyclist's silk balaclava, which I can pull up over my mouth and nose. In climates where it is extremely cold you can get neoprene facemasks which are even more effective. All these items are small and can easily be carried in a pocket. Similarly I carry a small pair of thermal gloves for when it gets very cold. Be sure, however, that your outer gloves are large enough because if they are tight, the thermals will have the reverse effect of cooling your hands by restricting the blood flow to them. When you have to take your gloves off for any reason store them inside your jacket to keep them warm and just before putting them back on blow into them – the effect is pleasantly surprising! I will talk further about extra equipment you may need for wilderness skiing in Chapter 5.

Boots

Boots, like shoes, are part of your clothing and again I would like to make a couple of points even though I may be talking to the converted. Comfort, even at this level of performance, has to be the most important factor, and if you have not tried the individually moulded footbeds that are commonly available, then I suggest you do so. Not only do they enhance comfort, but also they allow your feet to be more sensitive to the pressures under and around them, and this is essential to many of the new techniques with which you will be experimenting. Whether you favour a rear-entry or a front-entry boot is a personal matter, but whichever you choose it will probably feature a number of adjustments. Let me deal with these in turn.

Forward flex

This is the ability of the boot to bend as you subject the front of it to pressure by flexing your ankles forwards. Stiff ankles lead to stiff

Left: In bad conditions, protect yourself with good clothing.

actions; you need only jump up and down, trying to land cat-like, to confirm the truth of this statement. When you are skiing, however, the forces involved are much greater than when you remain on the spot, and the faster you go, the more they increase and the stiffer the boot needs to be. It follows, therefore, that a boot which offers a variable forward-flexing system is more versatile. You will have to experiment to find what degree of flexing you favour. It will depend on your weight and strength and the speed at which you ski, but remember it is the ability to flex the ankle that is important, not that it remains locked in a flexed position. You should constantly review this aspect of your skiing, because as you become more proficient not only will you end up skiing faster, but also your stance over your skis will change and your ankles will tend to flex less as you use the muscles of your lower leg to control the pressure distribution along the ski. At this stage you will need to stiffen and straighten your boots, but if you do so too early, you will tend to lose the sensitivity that is gained from having a soft flex.

Forward lean

Most boots feature an adjustment for altering the angle of the boot's cuff in the fore and aft plane, and the modern trend is to have this close to 90°. This position may well alter the way in which you stand on your skis, tending to promote a stronger, more upright stance and a style of skiing in which you roll your knees by rotating your femur in its hip socket. I explain this in more detail in the chapter 'Cruising with Style'.

Canting

Canting copes with the fact that most of us are to some degree at least either knock-kneed or bandy-legged. This is nothing new – Jean Claude Killy once called it his secret weapon. Not all boots feature a method of adjustment, and I suspect that if your boots require canting, it will have been picked up by now. If, however, you have not had your legs checked, it might be worth doing so. Most good boot retailers are able to do this.

Above: Rear-entry boots.   **Below: Front-entry boots.**

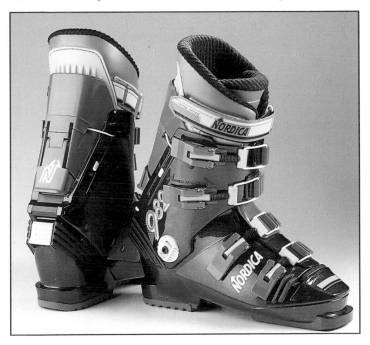

Bindings

Nothing promotes more confidence in your equipment than knowing it is safe to use. This is particularly so in the case of bindings, yet I am always surprised at how many people do not fully understand how they should be adjusted.

Manufacturers spend a considerable amount of time and energy ensuring that their bindings are as safe as possible. They also produce guidelines as to what setting you should ski on. These take into account a number of factors, including your weight or height, your skiing ability, the size of your tibia head and the sole length of your boot. By combining these factors they should come up with a setting that suits you. Make sure you consult their recommendations and know how to adjust your own particular binding. There are those who state that you can ski on very low settings if you are a good skier because good technique will not stress the binding. This is fine if you are 100 per cent certain you will not make a mistake and that your technique will always be perfect. If, however, you find that you are mortal and do make the occasional error, the binding will release and you will fall, possibly causing yourself unnecessary injury, whereas a correctly set binding will be more forgiving.

If you are going to buy new bindings, you will be faced with a massive choice. Every manufacturer assesses which type of fall (backwards, forwards, twisting or any combination) it considers to be the most common and then designs its release mechanisms around its conclusions. Alongside this it develops various aids to help you in and out of the binding and systems that allow for the flexing of the ski. By the time this book goes to press, a host of further features will probably have been developed. So how do you choose? I will try to answer this by considering which are the most important factors for skiers of advanced ability.

Elasticity

By this I mean the ability of the binding to partly release as a result of an overload and then to return to centre, providing the overload is insufficient to cause injury. The binding should release totally if injury would otherwise ensue. Good elasticity is of great importance and is a feature of all the top manufacturers' models.

DIN settings

There are now DIN standards for bindings to which every manufacturer has to adhere. They appear as numbers on the toe and heel pieces and tell you how tight the binding is. When you have worked out from the chart provided on which setting you should be skiing, check that the figure falls about halfway along the DIN scale for that model in order to make the most of the binding's elasticity. Not all bindings have scales that run from 1 to 10; many start at about 4 and go up to 15 or more, and the scales of racing bindings start and finish even higher. Finally, the settings work properly only if the action of the bindings is not impeded. To ensure this is the case, check the action each time you put on the bindings, especially that of the toe piece, as it can get jammed up with frozen snow or even grit.

Directions of release

Providing there is no loss in security, the more directions in which release can take place the better. Premature release is very dangerous, especially at the speeds at which you will be skiing as an advanced skier.

Ease of use

The ease with which you can put bindings on becomes a factor to be considered when you ski in deep snow. Some bindings are promoted as easier to handle under these conditions, which you may like to consider.

Maintenance

However good a binding, it only performs well if it is properly maintained, and fortunately this is done fairly easily. Keep bindings clean as grit and dirt in and around the moving parts not only wear them out but may actually hinder their performance. At the end of the season slacken off the tension screws, otherwise the internal springs will be continuously under pressure. Check if they are still greased inside and if not, regrease them with the correct grease. Do not use normal car grease as this hardens at the very low temperatures experienced on the slopes. If in doubt,

Below: This toe binding has been set on DIN 5.

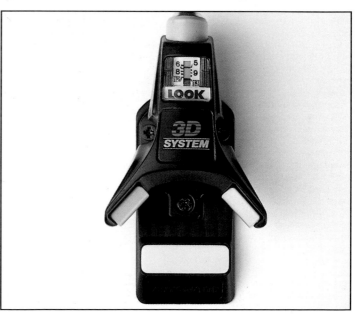

check with the binding manufacturer or retailer.

With correctly maintained and adjusted bindings you can feel confident about the skis coming off only when they are supposed to, which in turn can only help your skiing.

Skis

Good skis do make a difference. It is true that experts can ski impressively on anything but they would also be the first to agree that having the correct ski, that is well prepared, makes all the difference between success and failure. Giving advice on the choice of skis, however, is very difficult. I prefer to give the manufacturers the benefit of the doubt because if their marketing hype recommends a ski for a particular use and it turns out to be unsuitable, they have lost a customer, probably for good. It can only be to their advantage to recommend skis appropriate to the task. Ski magazines often run features on the latest models and are completely independent.

Remember that the all-round ski is really only ever going to be a dream or at best a compromise. The best powder ski will never perform as well on ice as a good slalom ski, for instance. Try to isolate those aspects of skiing you enjoy most and choose appropriately. For example, I prefer to ski powder and in the bumps, so I always favour a softer flexing ski that will turn quickly over one which will feel more stable at speed. If you have the opportunity to hire skis first, you will clearly be able to make a much better judgement when you come to buy.

Ski maintenance

Maintaining your skis properly is as important as choosing the right ones in the first place. The bases must be waxed correctly and the edges kept sharp. This is not as technical a job as you may first think, and all you need is a few tools and a work bench.

The first job is to clean the bases and de-wax them. Once this has been done, cut away any P-tex that is proud and clean out any grit from the gouges. If you have access to a

Above: Applying P-tex with a hot iron.

Above: Repairing with a P-tex candle, fast drip.

Below: Repairing with a P-tex candle, slow drip.

Above: Cleaning a repair and levelling the base.

Above: Hot waxing with an iron. Do not overheat.

Above: Sharpening the edges.

Below: Check the sharpness with your fingernail.

Above: Removing excess wax.

Below: Brush the wax for skiing in wet snow.

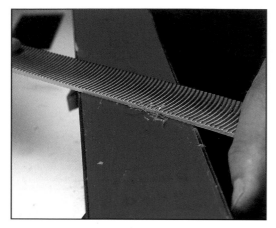

hot iron, use this to melt in fresh P-tex. Otherwise use a candle as a temporary measure – you can always clean out the sooty repair when you get home. Really bad gouges may require you to cut out a section and glue a new strip in place. As long as you cut an accurate template for the piece you are replacing, this is not as hard as you may think. If in doubt, however, most reputable ski shops are able to effect a good repair. When the P-tex has cooled, use a scraper or a radial file to remove any excess. At this point check the flatness of the base with a true edge and take off any further excess with either a metal scraper or a file.

With the bases flat it is time to tackle the edges. With a single-cut file the edges can be sharpened from the base and from the side. The angle between these two surfaces should be 90°, and it is possible to get edge-sharpening devices that ensure this angle is maintained. Many good skiers now prefer to sharpen their skis with a 1° bevel on them and achieve this with a special edge tool.

If you sharpen the edges along the whole length of the ski, there is a chance that you will feel the tip and tail catch as you turn. This can be avoided by dulling the edges in these areas. The length that you should dull can only really be found by experimenting and will be dependent on the side-cut of your skis. As a guide, start by dulling just the curve of the shovel and then about a hand's width back from the tail. Many skiers extend these distances on the outside edges of their skis so that they do not catch. This makes their skis right- and left-footed. As you become more proficient, the need to have your edges differentially sharpened in this way will become unnecessary and could even be to your disadvantage with some techniques. However, if the outside edges of your skis do consistently catch even when you think you are skiing technically well, it is worth trying this solution.

When you have finished sharpening the edges, use a stone to take off the small burrs that will have resulted from the filing action. It is

Above: A cold wax system that can be applied on the slopes.

worth carrying a small stone with you when it is really icy so you can hone your edges on the mountainside. You can tell if your edges are sharp by running a fingernail across them. If they are sharp, you will lose a small sliver of nail. Finally, go over the bases with a fine carborundum paper to prepare them for the next and final task – waxing.

Although there are a number of rub-on cold waxes available, I would recommend that you still hot-wax your bases and use hot waxes as your first line of defence. Occasionally conditions on the mountain change while you are skiing and it is then useful to rub on an appropriate cold wax. Hot waxes are available in a number of temperature ranges and although the universal grades are adequate for most conditions, it is worth checking that they cover the conditions you will be skiing in, especially if it is going to be very cold or very warm. The wrong wax can cause the snow to stick like glue.

The P-tex base is porous and soaks up the hot wax; it is therefore necessary to apply plenty and to iron it in sufficiently. The more the base soaks up, the longer it will last, but be very careful as the base will get hotter and hotter and there is a real danger of overheating, which will result in it delaminating. When the wax has cooled, you can either leave it on so that it will protect your edges from rusting during storage or, if you are about to ski on them, scrape it off. This

should be done with a plastic scraper and it is important to remove all the wax from the edges. If you are skiing in soft snow, the wax will last longer if you do not remove all of it from the surface. It is also recommended that you brush the wax with a nylon or bronze brush. This creates irregularities in its surface which prevent any suction developing between the snow and the ski base. On hard-pack, however, you must scrape the wax right down to the base and, finally, buff the wax with a cork or paper to give a really good finish.

Preparing your skis correctly will undoubtedly help your skiing, especially at this level of performance where you will be trying to get the maximum out of them.

Poles

The final piece of equipment to consider is your poles. First let us look at what length to use. Here we need to consider a number of factors – your style and level of proficiency, the type of terrain you want to ski and, of course, your body shape. If you ski with a very bent leg and a lot of ankle flex because you wear a soft boot, this needs to be taken into account. Stand in the position in which you ski and hold the pole by its basket end with your hand under the basket. In this position your forearm should be parallel with the ground. If, however, you ski more upright, as I will be encouraging you to do as you progress through the book, clearly a longer pole is necessary. You will need a longer pole also if you consistently venture onto steep terrain. Body shape plays an important role in that people have differing lengths of arm and differing widths of shoulders, both of which have a bearing on what pole length will work best for you.

A good pole plant is essential in many aspects of advanced skiing, hence it is important that your poles are easy to plant and do not get in the way. If you feel you are having to make odd body movements to accommodate them, it is likely that they are the wrong length, so experiment and be prepared to shorten or lengthen them appropriately.

BODY PREPARATION

As I sit here writing this section I am only too aware of its importance. I am absolutely exhausted after a mountain bike ride, a ride that is part of my pre-season build up. I could wait and simply go skiing when the first snows fall, and I am sure I would enjoy it, but I like to ski to a certain level and that requires that I feel my body is capable of the type of manoeuvres I wish to perform. I also feel much more confident knowing my body is well prepared and that it will therefore 'bounce better' if I fall. A fit body not only handles the skiing better but is less likely to be damaged because it is stronger and more mobile and fatigues less easily.

I am sure I do not need to convince you of these facts, but what I might need to do is to convince you that training can be fun – hence my bike ride. Mountain biking is an excellent medium for training because it not only develops muscle groups similar to those used in skiing, but it also develops balance. The point is that you do not need to sweat it out in a gym all the time in order to train.

At its best, training is very specific, which means that the movements involved should resemble those of the activity for which you are training as closely as possible.

Below: Mountain biking develops appropriate muscle groups and dynamic balance.

Take running as an example. If you use running to train for skiing, imagine every now and again that you are running through a slalom. This will encourage you to drive off the inside of your feet and strengthen muscle groups more appropriate to skiing than those worked by a normal run. You have to be imaginative in your training.

There are many books written about training, so all I will do here is outline the principles as they relate to skiing in order that you can apply them to whatever training regime you may choose.

Training should take place in three phases – the pre-skiing phase, the skiing phase and the post-skiing phase. Let us start by considering the pre-skiing phase.

Pre-skiing training

When you start depends entirely on how fit you are generally, but in order to make any significant improvements I suggest you allow at least three months. During this period you should tackle three areas of fitness: 1. endurance and stamina, 2. mobility, 3. power and strength. You should also build into your programme a variety of mental exercises. Remember that mental training is of equal importance to, and will need as much work as, your physical training in order to be effective.

1. Endurance and stamina

Muscular endurance is the ability of muscles to absorb and use oxygen and to dispose of waste products. Stamina is the ability of the heart and lungs to deliver this oxygen to the muscles and to remove the waste products from the system. Improving both has the added benefit of increasing your recovery rate, an important factor if you want to ski every day of your holiday.

There are two important factors to consider when planning a training schedule. The first is that you must work those muscle groups which you want to develop, and the second is that you must overload the system in order to produce results. The most important muscle groups are those of the legs, but you should not neglect the trunk, back, shoulders or arms (although

the last three of these are of less significance). To overload the system you need to raise your pulse rate into what is known as the training zone, and this is age dependent. Your maximum pulse rate is 220 minus your age, and your training zone is anything from 70 to 85 per cent of this figure. If you raise it higher than this, it will be less effective. You need to keep your pulse rate in the training zone for a period of about 20 minutes, and this should be preceded by a warming-up period and followed by a warming-down period.

The number of sessions you need to undertake will vary from individual to individual but on average will be something like three a week. It is important that you get the interval between these correct because if you train too frequently, you will end up exhausting the body's resources and your body will not have time to recover and change. (Training actually alters the organs of the body; for instance, the heart grows and new blood vessels are formed to cope with the increased demand for oxygen.) Similarly, if you train too infrequently, you will not improve. The best way to check if you have got it right is to measure your performance by recording your recovery rate. Every couple of weeks measure the time it takes for your pulse to return to its resting rate as soon as you have finished exercising. This time will shorten if you have the frequency of the sessions right.

2. Mobility

Unlike endurance and stamina training, you cannot do too much mobility training. It should precede all training sessions, but you should also have sessions devoted solely to stretching. The best way to stretch is known as slow stretching: stretch gradually to a point where you feel a slight degree of discomfort, hold that position for a count of twenty, then stretch a little further and count to ten. Your body should be warm before you do this and it is essential that you do not bounce into any stretches as this can easily cause injury. You should stretch every part of your body. There are many books on the market which give advice on stretching and illustrate the great variety of exercises at your disposal.

3. Power and strength

The principle of overloading but not overtraining applies equally to this aspect of training. As you become a better skier, so this area will become more and more important. Strength is the ability of a muscle to exert a force against a resistance, such as when you go round a turn. The faster you ski, the greater the force and the stronger your muscles need to be. Power, on the other hand, relates to the speed at which you can exert a force and cause movement to take place. It is important to the skier because it affects the speed with which the muscles can act. To be a good bumps skier, for example, you must have powerful muscles in order to react to the uneven terrain at speed.

Again the main muscle groups to concentrate on are those of your legs, your trunk and, as you become more able, your back, in particular the rotational muscles between your shoulder girdle and your pelvis.

These, then, are the main aspects of training you should consider before skiing. Be sure to consult the books listed in Further Reading (or others like them) before embarking on a training programme in order to reduce the possibility of injury and to maximise the return from the effort you put into your training.

Skiing training

This includes the training you do when you ski and involves almost entirely stretching and pre-ski

Useful warming-up exercises. Start gently, becoming more vigorous as you get warmer.

Top right: Leg raises.

Middle right: Jumping with both leg retraction and extension.

Bottom right: Trunk rotation. Rotate your poles at the same time to warm the arm muscles.

warm-ups. Ideally your day should start with a sequence of stretching exercises that takes in your whole body. When you get onto the slope, repeat enough of this to re-work the main muscle groups and then exercise these groups more vigorously to warm them up fully before actually skiing.

On my first run I continue to warm up by skiing in such a way as to test the conditions, my equipment and the way I feel. I work myself gradually into more advanced manoeuvres so that I experience success early in the day. If you throw yourself straight at the slope, you may not be sufficiently warmed up; consequently not only are you more likely to hurt yourself, but you will not feel as good about your skiing and may set a negative tone for the rest of the day. Be kind to yourself and set some easy initial goals so that you attain them and feel positive from the outset.

At the end of the day a good stretching session alleviates a lot of the aching you might be used to suffering. Saunas, hot baths, jacuzzis and even the disco can help your body relax and warm down.

Post-skiing training

When you return from your skiing trip, you may be aware of weaknesses in your fitness. You can plan specifically to improve these before you next ski. It is also worth noting that it is easier to maintain a level of fitness than to build it up, but I would guess that most readers of a book such as this are fairly athletic and active people anyway!

With mind, equipment and body prepared, it is now time to enjoy some 'fun in the sun'.

Top left: Back of the leg stretch. Stretch, count twenty, stretch further and count ten.

Middle left: Thigh stretch. Push the pelvis forwards, keeping the foot away from the bottom.

Bottom left: Inner thigh stretch. Do not stress the knee joint; if you feel any discomfort, STOP.

CHAPTER 2

CRUISING WITH STYLE

What is cruising with style? For me it is the feeling that I am descending the groomed slopes smoothly, in control and in a style that gives me pleasure. This style may not be technically the most efficient and it varies with my mood. Sometimes I get a kick from trying to ski with technical perfection; other times I like to ski with abandon, throwing classic form to the wind. On some occasions I go for speed, feeling the pressure of cold air against me, enjoying the adrenalin rush; on others I go for air time, leaping from every available launch pad. In my quieter moods I ski softly, delicately, disturbing the snow and the ambience of the mountains as little as possible. There are occasions when rhythm is the most important thing to me, when I enjoy the sheer pleasure of athletic movement; occasions when the edges are most important; and occasions when my concentration is taken up wholly by the environment around me, when the skiing becomes secondary to the delight I take from the mountains, the clouds in the sky, the forest glades, the jagged rocks and the crystals of snow over which I am gliding.

THE FUNDAMENTALS

I am able to enjoy this skiing freedom, however, only because I have learnt some fundamentals, some basic techniques which have developed into skills allowing me to realise my full potential on skis. It is these fundamentals that I want to make clear to you.

In the last chapter I spoke of the importance of dynamic balance. This remains the central constituent of the skiing freedom I have been talking about, but, although there is no substitute for constructive miles of skiing, there are a number of points, mainly to do with the posture you adopt, which will help you to develop your dynamic balance. Balancing on skis can be considered in three planes: 1. fore and

aft, 2. lateral, 3. up and down. When you practise, keep this in mind and improve your dynamic balance by experimenting with the degrees of movement possible.

Feet

Let us start by looking at the zone of contact with the snow – your feet. Most of your skiing so far has probably been done by balancing over the length of your foot, and this logically offers the most stable platform. In advanced skiing you will begin progressively to use different parts of the foot during each turn, which will enable you to use different parts of the ski. For this reason I will refer to the pressure you feel under your feet rather than talk of which foot you have your weight on – that is now too vague a notion to be of use. We will examine this matter in detail as we look at different ways of turning, but for the moment I want to concentrate on one of the biggest misconceptions held by many aspiring advanced skiers – that good skiers ski with their feet together.

The fact is that even though they may appear to do so, they don't in actuality. Let me explain. Find a polished floor and stand on it with

your stockinged feet about a hand's width apart. Now swivel your feet to your right until they almost touch. Your right foot will now be in front of your left by the same distance that originally separated them. Look at a picture of an advanced skier turning to the right (the skier's right as he or she descends the slope) and you will see that here, too, the right foot is in front of the left, and yet it appears that the feet are close together. What this amounts to is that you do not have to clamp your feet together in order to appear to be skiing with them together, and in fact to do so would severely hamper your development as a skier. Stand again on the polished floor in your stockinged feet, clamp your feet together and try to swivel quickly from side to side. The faster you move the more you will find yourself having to rotate your hips as well, and as your hips move so your balance will become more critical. Now try the same manoeuvre with your feet apart. You will notice

Below: Although the skier's legs are not far apart, skis and feet are not clamped together.

not only that are you able to rotate your feet faster and with more stability, but also that your hips remain relatively immobile. Furthermore, if your feet are clamped together, the leg on the inside of a turn will prevent you balancing completely over the one on the outside. But this is not the whole story of why you should ski with your feet apart, because an open stance has other benefits. To appreciate these we must consider the notion that it is desirable to ski almost entirely on only one leg through each turn. This is a theme I will be stressing throughout this section of the book.

In order to understand which leg we are talking about I will label your legs the outside leg and the inside leg of any one turn. The inside leg is that closest to the pivotal point of the arc of a turn, and clearly this changes from one turn to the next. It will be our aim to balance over the outside leg of any turn as quickly as possible, but why? There are two basic reasons:

1. With only one ski being sub-

Below: At this stage of the turn Alex's right leg is the inner leg and his left leg is the outer.

jected to the forces of the turn, it will bend into reverse camber more easily than if both skis are used. This is extremely desirable when you are trying to use the edges of your skis to the greatest effect.

2. Going from outside leg to outside leg as you change direction is generally stronger and more dynamic than involving the inside leg. To appreciate this, imagine yourself running in a straight line, turning to the left and then turning quickly back to the right. To do this you would need first to push off the inside of your right foot to go left and then off the inside of your left foot to go right. It is possible to perform the same manoeuvre by pushing off the outside of the opposite foot in each case but this is not such a natural movement and usually means crossing your legs slightly, something that is tricky when your feet are effectively two metres long!

Having established the desirability of skiing on one leg (the outside leg), it becomes necessary to stay on that leg until the next turn, and to do this we must not pressurise the inside foot. This is best achieved by keeping it in front of the outside foot, which, you will

notice, is in the same position as when we ski with feet apart. Skiing mechanics are extremely complex and what I have described here is again not the entire story, but I am ever wary of the stolen phrase I quoted in the first chapter – 'Analysis leads to paralysis.' Nevertheless, I hope I have convinced you that it is vital to ski with your feet apart.

Above and below: Runners tend to change direction by driving off the inside of the outside foot.

Ankles

It is now time to move up the body a little, to your ankles. In the first chapter I explained why I felt it important to have boots that allowed you to flex your ankles, and that stiff ankles could make for stiff actions. Let us now consider the effect of flexing an ankle on the rest of the leg. If you stand with your ankles bent forwards, you will notice that your knees also bend. This allows you to control the edges of your skis, which you do with your thighs and hips (more on this later). The alternative is to hold your ankles at an angle with your feet close to 90°. In this case it is a rotation of the thigh that controls the edges and your whole posture changes. As you will see, both techniques are acceptable. Furthermore, up to now you have probably controlled the fore and aft pressure on your skis by flexing at the ankle and pushing against the front of the boot. As you become stronger and more proficient, you will tend to use the muscles which run down the fronts of your legs to control the fore and aft pressure. This will transfer pressure muscularly rather than by shifting your balance.

Because of the need for flexibility in technique I suggest you experiment with both the flex of your boot and with its forward lean, gradually reducing the latter and adapting the former according to the type of skiing you are doing. Although a lower stance offers greater stability and is useful when you are experimenting with new balance sensations, it is not so appropriate for coping with changes in rhythm. In addition, it is more tiring and your muscles, therefore, are unable to act as effectively.

Knees

'Bend ze knees' is the oft-heard cry of the European ski instructors. We have seen that by flexing our ankles the knees automatically flex as well, but if we adopt a more upright position in our ankles it becomes necessary to bend at the knees. Bent knees are essential because only when they are flexed can we manipulate the edges of our skis and cross from one to the other. However, you should only flex them enough to edge the skis sufficiently for the turns you require. Approximately one per cent of your legs' strength is lost per one degree of flex on account of the loss of leverage entailed. A higher stance is both stronger and less likely to cause fatigue.

It is important that there is no twisting involved in the crossing-over action as it can cause damage to the ligaments supporting the knee joint. You will soon recognise whether or not you are doing this action correctly because you will experience a pulling sensation in the side of the knee joint when it is wrong. Stand without skis and experiment so that you can recognise the movement before you try it in motion. (It will not be exactly the same but close enough for you to feel if you are twisting the joint at all.)

There are two ways in which you can cross your knees over the line of the skis. The first is with your ankles flexed forward, which is probably the way most familiar to you. The second is performed by rotating the femur in the hip socket, a movement which can be felt best by sitting on a chair with your feet just off the floor and moving your feet from side to side as though they were a pendulum. This movement is possible when your ankles are at an angle of about 90° to your feet. Both movements will be useful to you.

Hips

The next area of the body we will examine is the hips and pelvis. It is a vital region of the anatomy in dynamic sports because it is where the upper and lower parts of our body are linked, and it is therefore essential that it complements the interaction of these two. To do this it must be unrestrained, yet with many skiers the opposite is the case because of the way in which they stand. I would like you to feel what I mean here, so stand up and hollow your back. Feel the tension this creates not only in the small of your back but also up the sides and maybe even in your neck and shoulders. Now from that position round the small of your back until these tensions disappear. What you are doing is tilting your pelvis upwards, and it is this latter position that you should strive for in your skiing. It allows you to use the power of your midriff without tensing other muscles and hindering actions that are taking place in the remainder of your body. Now you know the position I am referring to, try to jump and land softly in both

---

Below: Alterations to stance require changes in pole length. Be guided in your choice of poles by what feels right.

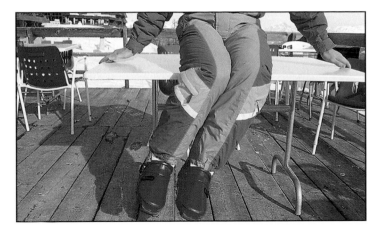

Above and below: Move the lower leg by rotating the thigh. Viewed relative to the ski, this action can be seen to entail crossing the knees over from one side of the ski to the outer.

see where you are holding your arms. This will be a good position to begin with. Second, the arms, via the hands, hold the poles and allow us to pole plant. It is important that the forces generated by the pole plant are transferred to the bulk of your body through your bone structure so as not to damage ligaments and tendons. To achieve this you may have to drop your hands slightly from their jumping position, making sure that the wrists are not turned out or in at all. If you have chosen your pole length correctly, you will be able to plant it from here with a wrist action accompanied by a subsequent lowering of the body by the legs. The simplest and best description of the position in which you will now find yourself is to imagine you are holding a hoop around your body with your hands at 10 o'clock and 2 o'clock (12 o'clock being directly in front of you). However, do not think of this as a fixed position but as one to which you return to find your balance. It will be valid as such even as your skiing becomes progressively more dynamic and you find your arms working as they do when you run.

The posture I have described, concentrating on different parts of the body from the feet up, is not to be rigidly held but should serve as the starting position from which your dynamic actions take place, and also the position to which you try to return after each action. From this position you will not only be able to develop your skiing skills, but also develop your own unique style according to the mood of the day.

It is now time to look at individual turns, but before we do so I must offer a warning. Most of your skiing will now be done at speed and it is essential that as your skill improves you develop an awareness of those around you. As an advanced skier you must avoid others and anticipate their actions. Remember the vulnerability you felt as a beginner when some supposedly advanced skier shot past only a hair's breadth away. A near miss is not enough – it shows poor skiing and a lack of skill. Give a wide berth to one and all as you enjoy 'cruising with style'.

positions. This should reinforce the need to tilt the pelvis upwards, the landing in that position being much softer and more controllable.

Head, arms and hands

It is a sign of an advanced skier that his or her eyes are kept level and focussed on where they are heading. Any swaying or tilting will upset your balance and lead to problems. The head tends to sway if you watch your skis or if you are tense. Free the tension and look ahead. When you are trying new manoeuvres, however, you may find yourself looking down at your feet to gain extra feedback about what is happening. Do not worry unduly about this as the tendency will soon

disappear as you become familiar with the new action. But do remember that your head can lead many actions, and that it is worth checking every now and again to see if you are actually looking in the right direction and that your head is leading you correctly.

Ski schools throughout the world keep coming up with different ways of describing where it is best to hold your arms, so let's start by considering what functions they serve. First and foremost they are agents of balance; whenever you try to balance you hold your arms out, usually slightly in front and to the side. Jump off a small wall or step and try to land as softly and as in balance as you can, then look to

FOOT-LIFTING TURNS

Sometimes, as you improve your skiing, you come across small 'skiing secrets', little techniques that seem to allow you to do what hitherto has been a mystery. Foot-lifting turns were certainly such for me, and now I'd like you to enjoy discovering them. What follows is

1

really a progression from a very basic technique right up to the most advanced movement sequences. The last are still being developed and refined by the world's top racers.

'Foot lifting' refers to the action that initiates the weight, or pressure, change from ski to ski at the start of a turn. For now I will leave the remainder of the turn for you to finish as you would normally,

3

although it is worth saying here that if you experience difficulty in linking these turns, it is most likely the result of not finishing a turn positively enough and you may have to read the next section in conjunction with this one. I am also assuming that you have mastered the fundamentals in that your basic posture is relaxed and that you feel ready to try something new. Foot lifting is a very simple, clean way to initiate turns that can be used in a variety of situations and is the first stepping stone towards cruising with style, but to start with it is necessary to find the right type of terrain on which to experiment.

5

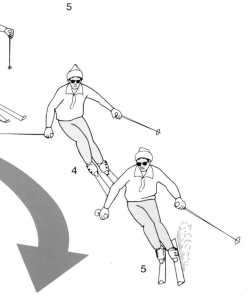

FOOT-LIFTING TURNS

Turn away from the fall-line (1), lift the outside foot (2) and THINK about where you want to go (3). Trust your body to look after the rest of the manoeuvre. As you replace the ski on the snow (4) and come around the turn (5), stay balanced over the new outside foot, feeling the pressure along the inside of it.

Terrain

You need to be able to ski quickly, but with no fears or inhibitions, so choose a slope that is wide, well prepared and relatively quiet: you do not want other skiers flashing past disturbing your concentration. After warming up, ski the slope a few times with your normal turns so that you are familiar with it and can ski it at full speed. You should then be ready to try the foot-lifting technique.

not worry. The correct procedure is to **plant** the pole and **lift** the foot simultaneously.

Coaching points

This form of initiation works very effectively in many situations and feels effortless because it makes use of gravity and your own momentum. It is the force of gravity which makes you slide down the slope, and when you offer resistance to it by making the edge of the

after the rest. Concentration on the one simple action of lifting your foot and on where you want to go is absolutely vital to the success of this manoeuvre, and adding anything else will just inhibit your chances of success. Your body has already learnt all the other actions – trust it to perform them.

Timing is critical so use your voice as a trigger. When you want to start the turn, shout 'Lift' to yourself (or out loud if it helps). If you are confused about which ski to lift, work it out before you set off then shout 'Right' as you start the turn to your right, then 'Left', and so on. This will both help with the timing and prompt you appropriately.

Be aware of the tension in your left thigh as you execute the first turn, and if you feel the need to sink on this leg as you go around the turn, do so; it will lead towards the next stage of development nicely.

Visualise yourself doing the manoeuvre, using the photographs and diagram to help you. Be committed: **lift** and go. Once you have done one you will have cracked it.

If it is not working or feeling good, consider the following:
1. Try going faster, as the turn only works at speed. Do not turn too much and thereby lose a lot of speed. Remember, it is important to have terrain on which you are comfortable at speed.
2. Lifting the foot is the very first thing you do. No stem is needed.
3. Be committed to making the turn, and trust yourself to complete it. A lot of positive visualisation is needed.
4. The first few attempts may feel uncertain and shaky, often the case when you try something new. Persist and you will become happier with it.
5. If you find that, having started the turn well, pressure builds up on the inside foot, you must slide it forward. A **lift** and **slide** action is required. Lift the ski then slide it forward during the turn, thereby ensuring that you do not pressure it.
6. If all else fails, take a good look at the fundamentals again. Return to enjoying a few runs down the slope, then when you feel relaxed and comfortable, try again.

Below: Choose a slope which is clear of other skiers and of a gradient with which you are happy. Try to do this when you are learning and practising any new manoeuvre.

Technique

This technique relies on you lifting the outside foot as you finish a turn. Start in the fall-line, pick up some speed, then turn gently to your left. As the turn takes you away from the fall-line, lift the right (outside) foot by retracting the leg and aim to go around a turn to your right at the same time. **Lift** and **turn**. You should need to do no more than *think* about making the turn and about where you want to end up next. As you cruise around the turn you can replace the right ski on the snow but *do not* put any pressure onto it. Now lift the left ski and cruise around to the left, now your right again, now your left. Build up a rhythm of turns, feeling how easy they are to initiate.

The pole plant is not really necessary for these turns, but if you find yourself doing it automatically, do

ski bite, you go around a turn, aided of course by the actions of your body. This resistance is normally created by the inside edge of the outside ski, and if you remove this, gravity and your momentum will tend to pull you down the slope again. When you lift your ski, you are removing the resistance; your body follows the flow-line, which tends towards the fall-line, your hip drops to the inside of the new turn, the pressure is automatically transferred to the left leg and away you go. The combination of all the movements that take place after you lift your foot is quite complex, and to think about these movements individually will only interfere with your ability to execute the turn; that is why it is important just to concentrate on where you want to be and nothing more – your previous skiing experience will look

Variations

Lifting just the heel of the foot, and thus the heel of the ski, gives you most stability but this movement is limiting. If you lift the whole ski, you have to balance over the whole foot. This is slightly more difficult but does encourage better habits so should be attempted soon after you have met with success with heel lifting. If you lift the toe or front of the ski, you will find that it tends to force you to use the tail of the ski and encourages you to slide the foot forward. It also encourages a shorter, sharper action, which is useful for turns down the fall-line. (Using the tail of the ski is a technique about which I will talk further later in the book.) Sliding the foot forward helps to release the pressure on it and encourages independent leg action.

The final variation involves just sliding the foot forward rather than lifting it. This is a more subtle version but works in the same way and is great for long cruisy turns that appear to happen by magic.

Foot-lifting turns are fine and, as I mentioned at the start, may be a complete revelation to you, but they are definitely just the beginning and I want to encourage you to greater things. You might justifiably ask why bother with them at all, but I believe they do have their place. There will be times, perhaps at the end of a long tiring day or on other occasions when your mood is such that all you want to do is to ski gently, when these turns are just what you need.

If I asked you to describe the turns, I am sure you would come up with words like *easy*, *relaxed*, *cruisy*, *coasting*, *effortless*, and indeed this is exactly right, but that's where the trouble lies. They are fine on long open runs where you want a wide-radius, effortless turn, but as soon as you demand more of your turning you will find they let you down. Try to shorten the radius and you will see what I mean – you will be forced to add movements. So let's use this turn as a basis and add to it.

Foot lifting with extension

Start by trying some shorter-radius turns. In order to achieve them I am sure you will find yourself having to stand up on your inside ski so that as it becomes the outside ski you are in a high, extended position from which you can sink and drive the skis around in a tighter arc.

Continue by thinking 'Lift and extend.' **Lift** the outside foot and at the same time **extend** the inside leg so you are in a more dynamic position and poised to dive around the turn. This action should come to you fairly easily, and I hope you will immediately feel a lot more power coming into your turns.

I am not going to allow you to rest here, however, because you will now be getting a hint of the real energy and control which it is possible to put into turning. Do not linger – this is just another stepping stone to greater things.

Before we look at how you are going to develop from here, I want to diversify for a moment or two and to try a couple of other ways of

---

Below: Lifting the whole foot.

Below: Lifting the toe, a help to independent leg action.

skiing. The turns I am about to describe are a lot of fun and will help to develop certain skills that are necessary to take the last turns further.

FOOT-LIFTING WITH EXTENSION

Below and bottom: Foot-lifting with extension. Adopting an upright stance as you move out of one turn into the next, with the inside leg extended as it becomes the outside leg, puts you in a position to sink and so drive your skis around the new turn more powerfully. Enjoy the sensation as a taste of improvements still to come.

By extending the inside leg as you approach the finish of a turn (2), you attain an upright position (3). From this you are free to sink (4) and maintain pressure on the ski as you drive it around the outside of the next turn (5).

3

5

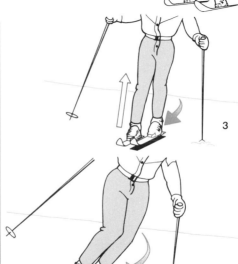

HIP AND KNEE CROSS-OVER TURNS

In every turn there comes a point at which you change your edges or cross over from that turn to the next. The actions we make to do this are always very similar but by concentrating on different parts of our body we get different results. Both the rhythm of turns and their radii can be affected.

One way of controlling the rhythm and radii of turns is to concentrate on the emphasis you place upon the use of either your hips or your knees in edging the skis. (To be exact, it is actually the thigh that controls this movement, although you may feel that the knee is directing operations.) Biomechanically this is a gross oversimplification because both are always involved, but by concentrating on one or the other you will get a different effect and I would like to stay with the philosophy of keeping things simple. Let's examine this difference by using two very simple ways of turning which I will call hip cross-over turns and knee cross-over turns. The 'cross-over' refers to the way in which your body crosses the line of the skis, thereby facilitating a change of edges. Both techniques rely heavily on rhythm in that it takes half a dozen turns before you begin to feel the effects, but once the rhythm takes over they are great fun.

HIP CROSS-OVER TURNS

Terrain
Use the same run as you used for learning foot lifting, or at least one of a similar gradient, and again ski it until you are feeling comfortable. Then find a section which is fairly even for a good distance because again you are going to be skiing at speed.

Technique
Before you start I want you to spend a moment or two trying to picture what is going to happen. See yourself going down the slope performing a series of linked flowing turns with minimal up and down motion of your body. Concentrate on your hips and notice how they apparently flow from side to side with each successive turn, crossing the line of the skis each time. This visualisation will not be precise because you do not yet know exactly what is going to happen, but it will help to focus your mind. With your mind concentrating on your hip region, it's time to go.

Head straight down the fall-line and when you have picked up speed, move your hips to one side. As soon as you feel the turn is established and your speed about to drop (which it will as you turn further from the fall-line), cross your hips over to the other side, which will cause you to turn that way.

Keep repeating this action until you feel the rhythm taking over. It is important that throughout you concentrate on your hips. The resulting turns should have a relatively wide radius and reasonably slow tempo. They are fast cruising turns which feel effortless.

Coaching points
Your voice can, as always, be useful to help with timing and to centre your mind on your hips. Feel as though your hips are staying at the same level off the ground throughout the run; it's not wrong if you find yourself bobbing up and down, merely a slightly different type of turn.

If you experience difficulty with these turns, consider the following:
1. You need commitment. If you hesitate at all in crossing your hips over from side to side, all is lost. Try the same manoeuvre but adopt a lower stance.
2. Remember rhythm – it is vital for overcoming any hesitation during the cross-over. You will only begin to appreciate the flowing nature of these turns after about the sixth one, so persevere.
3. You may find you are pressuring the inside ski during the later part of the turn. If so, slide it forwards during the turn and this will lighten it. Check your inside hip advances at the same time and that there is no twisting of the hips as you cross over from one turn to the next.

1

2

1

2

Top and above: Hip cross-over turns.

Left: In a series of hip cross-over turns a degree of up and down movement may occur naturally, although the action is best thought of as a smooth and level crossing of the hips over the line of the skis. This skier is moving between the two positions in the sequence depicted on this page.

HIP CROSS-OVER TURNS

The principle of crossing over is vital to advanced skiing and a secret to cruising with style. With these turns you simply concentrate on your hips, crossing them over from one side of your skis (1) to the other (2). Trust your previous skiing experience to take care of everything else.

KNEE CROSS-OVER TURNS

Knee cross-over turns require more effort than hip cross-overs and it is important that your legs are feeling strong and that you are fully warmed up. It is also essential that you know how to roll your knees from side to side without putting any stress on the ligaments, as I explained at the beginning of this chapter. If you have any problems with your knees, it would be wise to skip these turns until your legs are fully recovered. However, if you are fit and ready for them, they are a real joy.

Terrain

Choose the same run as before and just as you did with the hip cross-over turns I want you to spend a moment or two visualising what is going to happen. Once again, the purpose of this is to focus your mind, to centre concentration on your knees.

Technique

Picture yourself heading down the slope and then literally crossing your knees over to one side and then almost immediately back to the other, and so on in a fast rhythm. Your feet must be apart and, I repeat, there must be no twisting as you roll your knees, otherwise you are likely to damage them. Try the action standing on the spot as you visualise the turns and remember how it felt when you sat on a chair and swung your lower legs from side to side. Focus on this region of your body so as to improve your awareness of what is happening. This will not only improve your skiing responses but also help to protect you from injury, as you will feel much sooner when things are not right. When, through your imaging, you can sense your knees and lower legs flowing from side to side, it's time to go.

Point down the fall-line with your feet a boot's width apart and lower your stance a little. As you pick up speed, roll your knees to one side and as your edges bite, cross them back over to the other side. It will take quite a few turns before you feel the rhythm.

Above: Knee cross-over turns. A slight change of stance facilitates the rotating of the thighs and the crossing of the knees over the line of the skis.

KNEE CROSS-OVER TURNS

The squatting stance, thighs almost parallel to the ground and ankles at about 90°, allows the lower leg to swing from side to side.

Coaching points

The tempo is quite fast so use your voice to help. It will also help with your breathing, which can often get distorted in a sequence of turns with a fast rhythm. Eventually you should feel as though the skis are snaking from one turn to the next underneath you, that the edges of the skis are really biting and that it's almost as though the skis are turning themselves. If you are not experiencing these things, consider the following suggestions:

1. Exaggerate the cross-over action. The more you roll your knees, the more you will edge the skis and the more the skis will turn for you.

2. If the inside ski is catching or you are pressuring it, try lifting it slightly during each turn and sliding it forwards. Check that your inside hip is also slightly ahead of your outside hip.

3. If you find it hard to balance, lower your centre of gravity by adopting a lower stance and try again. These turns do require a little more perseverance than hip cross-over turns.

You may have noticed that I have not mentioned the pole plant again. This is because I feel the priority is what is happening to your feet and that is where your attention should be focused at this initial stage. If you find yourself doing one, however, that's fine as long as it feels natural. If you are not doing one, it is not vital and can be added later when you are feeling happier with the action of crossing over from one turn to the next. It may actually help quite a lot in the knee cross-over turns, especially if you have problems establishing the rhythm or are consistently finding it difficult to balance. In both cases the procedure is to **plant** then **cross over**, with a minimum of arm movement.

Variations

An interesting variation of the knee cross-over technique which produces short, sharp turns is worth trying. As you roll your knees, stamp down on the inside edge of the outside ski very firmly and repeat this immediately on the other side as you cross your knees over. The result will be a series of short, dynamic turns down the fall-line. You will also notice that your knees do not roll over as much as before and that you adopt a more upright position over your skis. As you perfect this technique, you will find that you are rebounding off each stamp and are able to ski the fall-line with short, sharp turns that almost squirt from one to the next. Although your speed will feel controlled, you will not be turning the skis very much, nor skidding them a great deal, as they are punched into the snow. This variation on the basic turn will prove very useful when you come to ski the bumps.

Having performed both hip and knee cross-over turns, let us now look at the differences between the two. The first thing that should be apparent is that the radius is different, the knee cross-over turns having a much shorter radius than the hip cross-overs. In addition, the rhythm of the knee cross-over turns is much faster. With the rhythm established, you should have no hesitation in flowing from one turn straight into the next. This crossing-over action with absolute commitment is the lesson I want you to learn from these turns, as well as the fun I hope they give you.

Below: By stamping down on the inside of her right ski Michelle has rebounded and is ready to repeat the action on the left.

TURN CONTROL

So far we have looked at several new ways in which to initiate turns but I have said nothing about controlling turns once they have started. Obviously at your stage of skiing you will have some of the necessary skills already, but now I would like to polish these because, clearly, to talk of turns only in terms of their initiation is going to lead to problems. As established earlier, advanced skiing is concerned with many interrelated factors of equal importance, including turn control. Let us start by examining the most common way in which we steer our turns; that is, in a way that slows our speed down.

First we need to examine what it is that controls the arc of a turn. Think back to the foot-lifting turns you tried earlier and recall what happened when you experimented with changing the turn radius, particularly as you made the turns tighter. The tighter they became, the more you found yourself bending and stretching. At the start of the turn you were in a high position, and then as you progressed around the turn you sank. All this happened without you really having consciously to think about it. Try it again but this time pay particular attention to what happens to your legs.

As you turn away from the fall-line you will feel the resistance under your outside ski building up. This will increase as you flex your legs (at the knee and ankle) and as you move your thigh inwards towards the centre of the turn. It is important that you move your thigh rather than twist your knee, which could damage it. The flexing of your leg must be done slowly so as to last the duration of the turn and it must involve your ankles, otherwise you will end up sitting back too much. Your shins should push firmly against the fronts of your boots, and you should feel this pressure building up. You are looking for the sensation that you can actually push and direct your skis exactly where you want them. It is a slow but powerful skidded type of turn. As you near the end of the turn

exaggerate the action of your thigh; this will have the effect of creating a platform under the ski (sometimes known as a check) which, depending on your speed, will either allow you to extend easily or, if you are travelling faster, actually cause a rebound from which you can initiate the next turn.

Coaching points

As we shall eventually see, there are many ways in which to finish turns but for the moment I would like you to concentrate on perfecting one. As you are driving the skis around the turn focus on your shin bones and feel how the pressure between them and the front of your boots builds up. It is often useful actually to grade this pressure from 0 – no pressure – up to 5 – pressure that can be sustained only by forcing your knees forwards. Being able to grade the response in this way will help you to experiment, and that is what you must do. No one can give you a hard and fast rule about how much pressure to put against the front of the boot, but the greater the pressure the more the action becomes defensive in nature. What you are aiming to be able to do is to steer the skis precisely in a variety of arcs. These arcs are dependent on the application of pressure, the rotation of your legs and, of course, the degree of edge you apply, which is controlled by the thigh of your outer leg.

The amount you edge, or tilt, the ski also affects the radius of a turn. The more you edge, the tighter the arc. Because of the waisting of the ski the tip and tail bite into the snow, allowing the middle to flex until the ski is in reverse camber, when the middle, too, bites into the snow. The more the ski is edged, the more the centre of the ski bends into reverse camber, which forces the ski to travel a tighter arc.

Learning to apply these points can be achieved only through structured practice, through going out on the slope and experimenting with turns of different radius. First, vary your turns by using different degrees of sinking and by sinking at different speeds and at different points during the turns. Perform

Above and below: The classic way of driving skis around a turn.

this sinking/flexing action first with your ankles, then with your knees and finally with both. See which is most effective in differing conditions. Remember it is possible to flex without exerting any pressure at all, so make sure your flexing actions do affect the pressure you feel under your feet.

Next, experiment with the distribution of pressure along the sole of your foot while standing still. Try it on the ball, along the inside edge and on the heel. Then vary the position of the pressure during a turn.

Now experiment with the amount of edge you use, finally linking all these elements together.

At your level of skiing this experimentation should not be difficult, and I am sure you will quickly master the art of steering your skis exactly where you want them to go. That is not the whole story, however; it is now time to take this skill further and into the realms of the advanced skier, because control does not have to mean slowing down. It can equally be the ability to increase your speed around a turn.

THE POWER TURN

I hope the experimenting you have just done will have increased your range of responses and reactions; this will now be very important. Up until now I suspect that most of the ideas I have suggested have worked fairly easily; those that follow may do so, too, but they will generally demand a greater degree of perseverance. In essence they are not complicated but they are subtle and require you to listen to your body, something which will inevitably take time to learn. What I can say to encourage you is that if you really want to become an advanced skier, these techniques will lead you there.

What, then, am I actually talking about? Basically we are going to look at ways in which you can add power to your turns. You can do this at three stages – at the initiation, during the turn and at the finish of the turn. Although I shall present the techniques relevant to each stage separately they should be considered together when you are practising, and it is only when you combine the three that you have 'arrived'. Those of you who have been skiing for some time may see similarities to the rotation and counter rotation techniques of yesteryear. They are, however, only similarities because these techniques are more subtle and far more powerful, making use of the entire body in a very dynamic way. Furthermore they are less contrived and more natural.

Terrain

As usual you will need to find a quiet run that is wide and friendly but just steep enough to demand that you control your turns and to allow you to ski it at speed. To ski it at speed is, in fact, the first thing I would like you to do. Paying attention to those around you, ski the run as fast as you can, and keep doing so until you are completely happy with your environment. This will achieve two things: first, you will become acquainted with the run and unfamiliarity with it will not then interfere with your future concentration; and second, by skiing at

your maximum speed for a while you will find when you do slow down a little that your awareness has improved and that you feel as though everything is happening considerably more slowly. This allows you to concentrate more easily on specific points.

Technique: the initiation

The initiation of your turns can be improved in two ways: the first is what I call dynamic stepping, and the second is a technique known as dynamic anticipation. The double use of the word dynamic will give you a hint as to what is to come.

Dynamic stepping

First I would like you to recall the foot-lifting turns we looked at earlier and in particular the development of the extension that was necessary in order to add power to the turns. We started by initiating the turns with a removal of the outside ski, which was achieved by lifting the foot. To overcome the limitations of this movement we added an extension of the inside leg at the same time. I want you to concentrate on the extension now rather than the foot lifting, first with short-radius, and then longer, turns. When you feel as though you are starting your turns by applying pressure to the inside ski, I want you to be aware of how you are applying that pressure, exactly where you are applying it and what follows immediately afterwards. This is a lot to think about, especially when presented in the form of the written word, so let me help you become more aware by asking a couple of questions.

As you extend your inside leg, where do you feel the pressure on the sole of your foot? When you extend, do you feel as though you are doing so upwards, upwards and backwards, upwards and forwards, to the side at all or any combination of these? For most of you the answer to the first question will probably be the outside edge of your sole. What I would like you to do is to move the pressure as quickly as possible to the inside edge of the sole and to feel as though you are driving into the turn

Above and below: Dynamic stepping and anticipation. Alex has carved around the bottom of the turn using the tail of his ski (1): he is straightening his right leg to maintain pressure and is beginning to drive into the next turn off the inside of his left ski. At the same time, his upper body is starting to wind into the turn. Committed to the inside of his left ski (2), he is also in a position to use all the muscles of his back and stomach to accelerate his skis powerfully around the turn.

off the ball of the foot. The movement is very similar to changing direction when you are running. This ties in with the second question, in that I want you to try to extend forwards and down the slope into the new turn. Both actions will produce the same effect; that is, a much more dynamic initiation and one which allows you to inject more energy into the turn. Your skis should be parallel or even diverging towards the tips during this manoeuvre, and if they are not, you need to concentrate on balancing on the outside ski and steering it powerfully around the turn. (See the next section, on dynamic anticipation, for help in this respect.)

When you are doing this movement correctly you will feel as though you are transferring from one turn to the next very quickly, and the reason for choosing the word dynamic will become apparent. From the moment you first recognise that the speed of the initiation has quickened it will become a matter for you to decide just how much energy you put into this action. The more energy you inject, the quicker the response.

Below: Dynamic stepping. Michelle is driving off the inside edge of her left ski (the outside ski of the new turn).

Coaching points

In some ways what you have been doing so far has been walking, and now you are learning to run. Foot lifting with extension was a walk, dynamic stepping is a run. The two actions are very similar but everything happens more quickly and dynamically in the second.

To try to analyse exactly what is happening would be detrimental to any attempt at performing the manoeuvre, and that is why I have been content merely to point you in a direction. Let us consider this direction further, however, and I will use the analogy of running and walking again.

When you walk, your legs almost seem to pendule from one step to the next; little effort is required unless you are walking quickly or uphill. When you break into a run, however, especially as you accelerate, your muscles feel as though they are constantly under tension, the action of one leg complementing that of the other. It is also not unlike a pedalling action. Dynamic stepping is the same.

Imagine that you are about to turn to your left, that your left foot is currently the outside foot and your right foot the inner. As the turn you are on finishes, all the tension is in your left leg. You straighten it to keep the edge of your ski biting but as you are doing so your right leg also tenses and straightens, projecting you forwards and down the slope into the next turn. Both legs are involved in this action simultaneously (certainly as far as you will be aware).

As I said at the start, this is a subtle action insofar as it will creep into your repertoire after much perseverance rather than land there with a bang. So how do you know whether you are doing the right thing? If by following the above advice you find that your turn initiations feel quicker, that the edge is biting much sooner and the ski is reacting more positively than previously, then you are heading in the right direction. Dynamic stepping, however, should not be tackled in isolation but practised alongside the next technique, that of dynamic anticipation.

Dynamic anticipation

This is one of the most important factors in advanced skiing and like dynamic stepping will require some dedication on your part. Again it will probably creep into your technique rather than arrive with a bang. Do not be daunted, however; if you have got this far, you will certainly be able to handle it.

Terrain

You will need to find a slope that is steep enough for you to feel as though you just about need to control your speed. It should be smooth, wide and free from anything that may distract your attention.

Technique

I am going to approach this technique from two different angles. If you gain success from one method I would like you still to try the other as I think you may yet discover something new about your skiing.

Method 1

The turns you will be doing are medium-radius turns that are linked rhythmically yet turn sufficiently to allow you to maintain control. The object is to inject some of your own energy into the turn and to accelerate your skis around the arc. This is not actually a contradiction because although you will be turning quickly you will still feel in control. The difference is that up until now you have been slowing down slightly as you have turned away from the fall-line, and now you will be using the power in your body to accelerate the skis around the latter part of the turn or at least to reduce the slowing down to a minimum.

Having initiated the turn with dynamic stepping you will feel as if your skis and legs have been left behind. Concentrate on the outside of your body, your hands, arms, shoulders, hips and thighs, and as you go around the arc of the turn try to accelerate the skis by driving your legs forwards. Your pelvis and upper body will feel tight because you are working all their muscles in

---

Right: Dynamic anticipation. The shoulders lead, allowing the rotary power of the back and stomach to drive the next turn.

unison. It is not a restrictive movement, however; the body is not locked or blocked by it. I sometimes lead the movement with my hand, imagining that it is attached to my hips with a short length of rope. The pole plant results from a swinging action at the wrist that is in time with the rhythm of the turns. The action will cause your body to become squarer over your skis at some points in the turn than you might be used to, and if you take it too far, the tail of your ski will eventually break away. Timing is critical. Concentrate on the whipping-around action as you start the turn but then prepare for an early pole plant almost immediately you come out of the fall-line. Try to lead into the pole plant with your shoulder girdle only. This will cause you to twist your upper body at the end of the turn. Think of your body as two blocks, your shoulder girdle and your hips, which are linked by a powerful spring. As you pole plant, your shoulder block will anticipate your new direction but your hip

The hip block catches up with the shoulder block (1, 2, 3). The pelvis and legs continue to drive the outside ski forwards (notice the use of the back of the ski) while the shoulders anticipate the approaching turn (4). The spring coils and is ready to be released (5).

DYNAMIC ANTICIPATION

block and legs will continue to drive around the arc, and so the spring will be wound up. As you initiate the next turn the spring's energy will be released and you will add power to your turn.

'How is this different from classic anticipation?' you may be asking, and indeed in some ways it is similar. With classic anticipation the spring is much shorter and joins your hips to the bottom of your rib cage, altogether a much weaker arrangement. Because it is weaker

4

it is easier to wind up, and you tend to do this right at the last moment with a sudden twisting downhill of the whole of the upper body. It is a useful technique but it does have its limitations. Dynamic anticipation involves, as we have seen, a much longer spring which requires constant winding up throughout the turn. You will certainly feel the difference when you get it right; your turns will feel more powerful throughout.

Coaching points

Remember that you are trying to accelerate the skis around the turn and that this involves an expenditure of energy. You should feel tired after trying it! Allow your body to follow its flow-line and, making full use of its momentum, force your feet and skis to keep up with it.

Concentrate first on the wind-up by driving the skis around with the whole of your body, paying particular attention to your hips and pelvis. Your pelvis will have to be tilted as I described at the beginning of the chapter. Do not worry if you find the skis breaking away at the end of the turn; in fact it is a good thing to take them that far a few times to find out just where they do break away and then to initiate the next turn just before that point.

When you feel you are accelerating the skis successfully, start to concentrate on the pole plant. Try to lead with the shoulder girdle only, though I suspect you will feel everything is happening so fast that initially you will not be sure exactly what is what. Experiment by altering the way you pole plant until you notice a quickening in the speed with which you go from one turn to the next. Also, feel your torso actively involved in the turning process; at the moment you plant the pole your body should feel at its most powerful, coiled and ready to unleash its energy into the turn.

Method 2

Up until now you have been concentrating on the way in which your legs steer the skis, but now I want to move the centre of concentration to a point just below your belly-button, to your centre of mass, the midriff region of your body (you did

this when you tried the hip cross-over turns). This is the real power centre of your body. The sensation you are looking for is that the power has moved away from your legs up to your midriff. The muscles here are firm but flexible. They are relaxed in the sense that they are being actively used but are not tight and thereby locking the upper body to the legs. Your pelvis is

THE POWER TURN

The outside of the body is accelerated around the turn (2). It is as though you feel all the power being directed from the centre of the body (3).

Above right and right: The power turn. In this sequence Megan is driving the outside ski powerfully around the turn. Her inside arm has dropped back, an indication that the right-hand side of her body is moving forwards relative to the left. Her timing is perfect: if she took this movement any further, the ski would break away.

1

3

tilted upwards, which releases the muscles from any blocking actions. (Remind yourself of the exercise you did earlier of hollowing your back then relaxing it.) It is from this power centre that I want you to feel you are steering the turn. It is almost as though this point of your body is the pivot of the turn and your legs follow an arc around it. (Clearly this is impossible but the sensation is of this happening.)

Try to visualise the path these turns will take. I want you to imagine two lines on the slope, the line your skis follow and the line your power centre follows. The power centre follows the flow-line of the turn and your skis run around a series of wider arcs. As your skis turn away from the fall-line at the end of the turn, pole plant. Your power centre immediately redirects itself towards the new turn (any hesitation and the effect will be lost) and pulls the skis around the new arc, accelerating them so they can keep up with the rest of your body. The suddenness of this action disappears as the rhythm of the turns takes over, and it is vital that it does so because what you are experiencing is a constant twisting and untwisting of the lower body relative to the upper body; there is no passive moment in the entire procedure. Your upper body will always be turning just before your skis, just as you would expect from the lines you visualised.

Coaching points
Although this last description may sound a little vague, it does in fact outline the way in which I get myself to perform this technique. Feeling that the power is coming from the centre of your body is a great sensation because not only do the muscles you are controlling feel so much more powerful, but it also feels so much more stable.

Which ever way you approach power turns it is important to continue experimenting with them at various speeds and with differing radii. The techniques I have described will enhance almost any turn and will, I hope, occupy a prominent place in your repertoire from now on.

FOOT THRUSTING
Foot thrusting is another very useful technique that can be applied to a variety of turns in order to add power to them. It is not one you will always use, nevertheless it should definitely be a part of your repertoire, so much so that you are able to apply it spontaneously as the occasion demands. It allows a cleaner transition from edge to edge and makes more use of the tail of the ski. It is the tail that holds best at the end of a turn. The technique is of particular value to those who constantly find their skis skidding excessively towards the end of a turn.

Terrain
Return to the slope on which you practised hip cross-over turns.

Technique
During a series of hip cross-overs I want you to focus on the pressure under your feet throughout a single turn. Initially I suspect you will feel it is fairly constant along the whole inside edge of your foot, but now I want you to experiment with shifting it from one end to the other. As you start a new turn feel the pressure at the front of your foot, and as the turn progresses around its arc feel the pressure move back until it is along the length of your foot and finally, as you complete the turn, feel it on your heel. This is different from leaning back, when you would feel the back of your leg against the boot. In this case you should only feel pressure under the heel. What you are in fact doing is using the whole edge of the ski to the greatest effect by thrusting your feet forwards during the turn. It is different from the technique of dynamic anticipation because here we are concentrating on moving the lower leg only.

As the next turn starts you may have to project yourself forwards again so that you start on the front of the ski and are able to repeat the sequence, though this will tend to happen naturally anyway. Initially you may find that you do end up leaning too far back, but with practice you will soon judge it so that you gain the greatest amount of grip from the tail of the ski without losing your balance.

Foot thrusting can be applied to many turns and it will certainly increase your versatility if you are able to use it at will. When you are quite happy with it, try applying it to the power turns dealt with earlier. This should not prove difficult as the movement lends itself well to the whole action.

Once the difficult concept of the last few pages has been assimilated, you really will be 'cruising with style'. If it all seems too much, do not despair; tackle each stage in turn and practise with patience.

FOOT THRUSTING

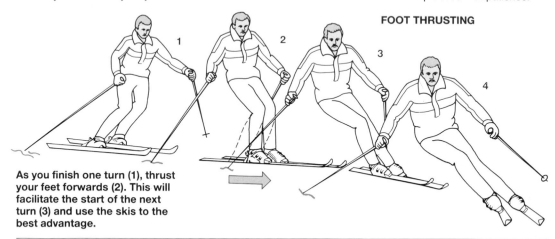

As you finish one turn (1), thrust your feet forwards (2). This will facilitate the start of the next turn (3) and use the skis to the best advantage.

STEP TURNS

In this final section on cruising with style I would like to introduce two more advanced turns which bring together all the skills you have been developing and which are also great fun. They belong to a family of turns known as step turns, and I will cover the remainder of the family in a later section where we will be applying them to more difficult snow conditions. They are different from the dynamic stepping action in that they include a gliding phase.

Parallel step turn
The parallel step turn is very much as its name implies and has come, as has so much advanced technique, from the world of racing. It is a fast turn so choose a slope where you can ski comfortably at speed.
Technique
Start with some wide-radius turns, then when you are going fast, step from the inside edge of the outside ski (by straightening that leg) onto the outside edge of the inside ski. You will now find yourself on the outside edge in a fairly upright position. Glide for a moment, then with a downward flexing motion launch into the new turn. You will now be able to use it at will. When you are on the inside edge of the same ski. This last movement should not cause any problems if you have managed everything up to now; it should be just as though you are swooping down the slope.
Coaching points
The most important phase is again the finish of each turn, because it is at this moment that the platform on which you stand up is formed. Without that the turn will be very weak. As you are about to step, sink down and drop your thigh in a little further, thus helping to create a firmer platform.

As you step up onto the outside edge of the other ski, do not rush to go into the next turn. Use some words to help with the timing, e.g. 'Up aannddd sink.' As you sink and flow into the new turn there is a strong sensation of swooping down the slope, which is one of the reasons this turn is so much fun. Racers use this technique to adjust their line to the next gate. As an advanced recreational skier use it whenever the mood takes you!

Scissor step turn
This turn is really only a variation on the last, and is sometimes known as a racing step turn. Start as before but this time, instead of stepping the ski up parallel, open the tip out just as you would when skating. Having established your balance over the new ski, again launch into the new turn by rolling your hips and thighs towards the centre of the turn. The skating or scissor action allows you to power into the turn on a slightly refined line and actually to accelerate, which is one of the reasons racers use it. The more powerful you make the skating action the more fun the turn becomes.

If you have mastered all the techniques covered in this chapter, the chances are that you are technically an excellent skier, but it is only when you are able to apply them with skill to all the subtle nuances of a slope that you can be said truly to be 'cruising with style', and perhaps of more importance cruising with your own individual style.

Right and far right: Scissor step turn. This variant of the step turn is but one among many you can choose to adopt. Notice how the skier is driving forwards onto the new ski.

PARALLEL STEP TURN

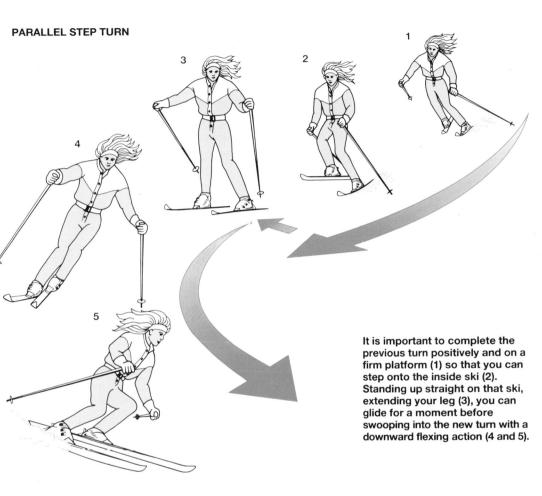

It is important to complete the previous turn positively and on a firm platform (1) so that you can step onto the inside ski (2). Standing up straight on that ski, extending your leg (3), you can glide for a moment before swooping into the new turn with a downward flexing action (4 and 5).

CHAPTER 3

RIDING THE BUMPS

When I first decided to call this chapter 'Riding the Bumps', a very knowledgeable ski-instructor friend said, 'You can't call it that. Bump skiing isn't passive.' He had related 'riding' to riding in a bus or car, whereas I was relating it to riding a horse, a bike or a surfboard, and in these cases the riding is far from passive. At the same time it is more than the mere exertion of a force over something impassive. It is the harnessing of a force, and entails interacting with that force. A horse rider works with the horse and surfers use the energy of the waves; they do not fight them. Bump skiing is much the same. Good bump skiers play with the interaction of gravity, the bumps and their skis. The bumps are their friends and help them. In the following pages I hope to make them your friends as well.

There are many techniques that can be of use in bump skiing, and the expert skier will use a combination, reacting to the ever-changing slope. Knowing this, however, is not of much practical use to you because it is impossible to learn all the variations and subtleties at once. You need to work on them individually and then as soon as possible blend them together into the type of bump run to which you aspire.

This last is an important point. Just as with cruising you may find there is a level at which you turn round and say 'No more.' So be it. Skiing is fun and you should not feel under any pressure to try it in a way that is not you. That 'you' may change as the years and ski miles go by, but it is how you feel at the moment that is important. With this philosophy in mind I have called the various techniques by some odd, perhaps even slightly glib, names, in an attempt to capture their feeling and mood. They do not need to be learnt in any special order; it will depend upon the terrain at your disposal and your prevailing mood as to which you decide to practise.

You have to start somewhere, however, so try to choose a reasonable slope. Verbier's Tortin or Killington's Outer Limits would definitely be jumping in at the deep end. What you need is a gentle slope with reasonably soft snow and some bumps. Ideally it should not be too long and should have an easy run-out not only at the bottom but also, if possible, at either side. Such perfection is not common so seek out the slope that comes closest. Whatever you settle on must not be intimidating.

THE SMOOTH WAY

I have called it the smooth way because the action I want you to consider is, effectively, one of smoothing out the terrain. The upper body stays at a level while the legs go up and down, absorbing the bumps. It is an extremely important technique to add to your armoury, not just for the bumps but also for many other situations that you will come across as an advanced skier.

The skill of absorbing Terrain

Find a bump field which meets the criteria I have already mentioned.

Technique

Traverse the bumps, slowly at first, absorbing them by allowing your legs to bend under tension so that as you come off a bump they automatically spring back into the hollows. To understand this action hold your arm out horizontally and get a partner to apply pressure to your hand. Gradually, as the pressure increases, let your arm bend while maintaining a degree of resistance. Tell your partner to release the pressure by removing his or her hand but to do so without any warning, and observe what happens. When the pressure is removed, your hand will shoot forwards just as a compressed spring would. This is the reaction you want

Left: Riding the bumps.

from your legs as you go through the bump field. Your upper body should remain at the same level throughout. As you become more confident, steepen the traverse angle. You may even be able to practise in the fall-line in a small bump field.

Coaching points

It may help to imagine you are balancing a book on your head or carrying a tray of glasses. Pay attention to the pressure under your feet and try to keep it constant. Focus on something ahead so that your eyes remain steady. If you keep looking at a bump as you approach it, your head will drop forwards and this may lead to you bending too much at the waist. Exercises like this help to keep the upper body quiet and give you feedback as to whether you are succeeding.

As you reach the crest of each bump, breath out forcibly. The value of breathing correctly is immeasurable in bump skiing. You can use your voice to help with this. Choose a word that describes the action and one which is naturally said with an expulsion of air. I like the words *fold* and *bend,* for example. As you approach a bump say

the word, extending it so it matches your actions: 'Foooold.'

Plant your pole just before the crest of each bump, and as you go over, assuming the bumps are quite large, your head will normally be level with your hand.

Remember that as you come off a bump you have to extend your legs back into the trough in order to keep your body at the same level and to allow your legs room to retract over the next bump.

At the top of each bump feel the tension in your thighs and stomach.

Throughout, your back should remain at a constant angle so that it is your legs that do the absorbing. This point is very important, and will become increasingly so as you ski the bumps faster and steeper.

When you are completely happy with the way in which you are absorbing the terrain, it will be time to try some turns.

ABSORBING THE TERRAIN

The legs flex to smooth out the undulations, giving the body a quiet, almost level ride.

them using this technique a great deal. Their upper bodies appear still and all the movement occurs (or appears to occur) below their knees. You will also notice that they do not deviate from the fall-line.

Coaching points

One of the things that may strike you as you experiment with these turns is that you are travelling very quickly down the hill because you have to ski the fall-line. At first this will be disconcerting because you will feel that you are continuously accelerating; if you persevere, however, you will notice that your speed reaches a point at which it steadies out. It is as though you have moved up a gear and reached a new cruising speed beyond which you do not accelerate. Your speed is controlled by the stamping/ checking action. Think about this taking place halfway round the turn

rather than at the end. Do not be tempted to turn too much as this will interrupt your rhythm.

There is much debate amongst bump skiers as to whether you should start standing tall or in a low position. My own preference for these turns is a high position, but there are also techniques in which I do employ a low start position. There are so many individual factors involved that I suggest you find out which works best for you by experimenting with both stances.

The pole plant is absolutely vital in these turns and requires practice on an even slope. The more confident you are of being able to do them there, the more chance you will have of performing successfully in the bumps.

Use your voice to help with your breathing and timing, which again are crucial in such short-tempo turns.

THE WILD WAY

I use the term 'wild' in the sense of exciting rather than crazy. This is my favourite bumps technique but I confess that I have to be going well for it to work. I have to be feeling strong and in need of an adrenalin buzz. I am not trying to put you off – on the contrary –, it is just that unless you are in an appropriate mood it will not feel right.

The idea itself is simple. You are going to do knee cross-over turns through the bumps, adapting your rhythm in accordance with the dictates of the bump field. It is the rhythm that is important, the line being only secondary. The turns use the edges to the maximum, and you need to absorb the terrain completely and spontaneously at speed. This might sound daunting but by this stage of the book you will have acquired all the necessary techniques. All you need do is apply them skilfully, and provided you choose appropriate terrain you may well surprise yourself.

Terrain

The ideal spot is a moderately steep bump field with a gentle run-in and some form of easy run-out, either to the sides or at the bottom.

Technique

Start your turns well before the bumps so that your rhythm is established by the time you hit the first one. The secret is to maintain continuous edge contact, and to achieve this you will have to be absorbing well. I find a low stance useful on this occasion because it enables me to really edge the skis, but it is essential that you extend well into the troughs otherwise you will run out of leg room on the top of the bumps. Each leg needs to be acting independently, and you will find there are occasions when one leg is in a trough and the other is going over a bump.

Coaching points

Keep your arms well forwards and wide apart. If you let your arms swing in at all, as they easily can do with a strong rhythmic turn, they will block you.

Above: Riding the bumps the sharp way. Michelle's left ski has checked on the back of the bump, and she is already using her right ski to steer towards the trough. The ideal line follows the troughs but, of course, bump fields are never that well designed and in fact Michelle has had to absorb the bump as well, thus combining the sharp way with the smooth way.

Left: Can you see the obvious line? Being able to read the bumps comes with practice and concentration.

Imagine yourself doing the run, not down a specific route because the line is hard to predict, rather with an emphasis on the rhythm of your movements and the sensation of the skis flowing beneath you from side to side.

Control your rhythm with your breathing, particularly during the expulsion phase, when words and sounds can lend emphasis to the action.

For most of us there is definitely a limit to the steepness of terrain through which we are capable of doing these turns. Have the wisdom to be honest with yourself and to bow out gracefully when you realise it has become too much. That is not negative thinking; on the contrary, it is very positive because you will have recognised your limitations and acted according to reason, not under pressure from irrational fears.

Above and below: The wild way. Rhythm dictates the line, and the skier absorbs the bump while carving over the crest.

THE CRAZY WAY

Every now and again you will see skiers crashing straight down the fall-line of a bump field, slamming into the backs of the bumps. This is the crazy way. It can look great, but I have chosen my description carefully because not only do you need a slightly crazy attitude of mind to ski in this manner but it is a sure way to ruin your knee joints. I recommend that you do not ski this way but the choice must ultimately lie with you, that is why I am describing it.

Terrain
The bumps should be steep but with soft backs.

Technique
Your legs need to be strong and thoroughly warmed up. The technique is basically very simple. Instead of heading for the valleys start on top of a bump and head for the crest below you. As you hit it, extend your legs sharply and momentarily, which will check your speed slightly. The force will be

sufficient for you to absorb the bump after this extension, and you then head for the next bump.

Coaching points
Don't do it! Just occasionally, however, knowledge of this technique may be useful. It is the short extension which will slow you down and as long as it is immediately followed by a collapsing of the legs you will not become airborne. This kicking action pushes your heels into the snow, sometimes with a flat ski and sometimes on the edge, depending upon whether you want to turn or not.

Your pole plant should coincide with the kicking action.

Below: The crazy way. Here the skier is crashing into the tops of the bumps. As he does so, he remains centred over his skis and does not break at the stomach. The faster he goes, the more he will be able to ski from crest to crest, which will reduce the stress on his knees; however, they are still at great risk.

THE SMART WAY

You have practised all the techniques and are at the top of your favourite bump run. You have been performing hard and fast on the groomed slopes and are feeling really good about your skiing. Ahead lies a maze of well-formed bumps; the snow is soft and you know you are about to enter the fun zone. In your mind's eye you can see yourself riding the bumps, and you can feel the rhythm.

As you look down the slope a line becomes clear, at least as far as the fourth bump. It is enough to get you going. You relax yourself by controlling your breathing, and then you're away.

The first bumps flash by as you ski the valleys, checking your speed with small heel thrusts. The rhythm is short and sharp; you are in control and add a couple of wiggles. This is great. Suddenly a bump looms right in front of you.

You fold as you hit it, knees reaching your chest, and the pole plant is solid. The arc of your turn remains uninterrupted. Another bump follows but you handle it and are still in control. It's time to rev up. Diving into the valleys you feel the smoothness of the snow as your skis snake around the trough with no braking effect. Your legs feel fluid. At the end of this valley system you can see another big bump, a perfect launch pad. Hitting it squarely you take to the air and tuck. Holding the tuck just long enough to clear the next bump, you extend your legs and your skis land on the down-side. A quick, short, sharp turn puts you back in line. Ahead the slope shallows slightly; you roll your knees and feel the edges bite. The skis climb the back of a bump and you roll your knees to the other side, absorbing at the same time. The rhythm comes – turn, turn, turn. Your upper body is quiet; your legs work smoothly be-

low you, flowing from side to side and absorbing whatever they cross. This is the vision, this is what you have been working for, linking everything together automatically, acting and reacting to the playground. Ahead the slope steepens again. Relishing the increase in speed you . . .

A run like this is within your grasp. It's the smart way to ski the bumps, knitting all the techniques together into a great run; choosing how you want to ski it and yet being able to cope when, as in all great runs, the slope throws in something unexpected. Bump skiing is one of the great challenges of advanced skiing, and in the same way that a true mountaineer never accepts that he or she has conquered a peak, merely climbed it, so you, an advanced skier, should accept that, although you may have many great runs under your belt, somewhere there is still a bump with your name on it. But that's all part of the fun!

Far left (top and bottom) and left: The smart way. In this three-picture sequence Fred is employing a combination of techniques to ride the bumps. It is certainly the versatile and inventive skier, able to draw on a reserve of varied skills, who fairs best when faced with the irregularities and surprises which are common to all major bump fields.

Right: The tuck jump. Jumping is something many skiers wish to be able to do, and feeling comfortable when airborne is important for the advanced skier. The bumps are a great place to start getting the feel of being airborne as they are natural take-off ramps. Good skiers often jump from one bump, fly over the next, and land on the down-side of the one after; and of course there are a myriad tricks for the accomplished practitioner to perform. Initially, however, I suggest you stick to tuck jumps and make sure the landing is soft and sloping downhill.

CHAPTER 4

SKIING FOR ADVENTURE

One of my favourite personal skiing stories concerns a dream I once had high up on a snow-covered ridge in the Himalayas. I was close to the tree-line in snow leopard country, and as I lay on a sunbaked rock taking in the atmosphere of this special place, I started day-dreaming. In my dream I was joined by a beautiful snow leopard, and together we plunged down through the powder, exploding in and out of its softness, my turns matching its leaps. I often leave the listener in doubt as to whether or not it *was* a dream. It is never my intention to mislead, but I make no apologies because the powder is the stuff of dreams and adventures: everyone's memories of a great powder day are a mixture of fact and fantasy.

Although some advanced skiers aspire to crash through the moguls or to win the slalom race, I think it would be fair to say that every skier would like to ski the powder well, to leave his or her signature on the white expanse, to find that untouched, virgin slope. When you

are finally confronted by such a slope, you will appreciate one of the reasons why I have called this chapter 'Skiing for Adventure'. The excitement and the thrill lie not only in the act but equally in the anticipation of the act.

The concept of an adventure is important because, although much is written about the beauty of powder, the reality is that once you venture away from the prepared and patrolled areas the rules change dramatically. In the first place, the freedom to ski where you like varies from area to area, and it would be irresponsible, and in some cases illegal, to ignore the recommendations of those that control the ski areas. Secondly, the terrain demands a greater understanding, a closer empathy from you. The snow is not always deep, soft and friendly; it is frequently hard, crusty and even sticky. There is the ever-present threat of avalanches and of bad weather. And in most areas you have to be totally self-sufficient and independent of the rescue services. In return, however, the rewards are second to none, and if you educate yourself in the necessary skills, you will not only be able to move in safety but of equal importance you will be able to move in sympathy with the environment, something especially desirable since the winter ecology is delicately balanced and can so easily be upset by your presence. An understanding of mountain lore is necessary not just for your safety but also for the protection of the flora and fauna that exist in these harsh but splendid surroundings. For this reason I insist that this chapter, which will teach you to ski not just the powder but all the crud as well, is read in conjunction with the next, called 'Mountain Lore'. Only then will you understand truly how to 'ski for adventure'.

Left: Smooth, soft snow, breathtaking scenery, a beautiful day – the greatest adventure skiing has to offer.

Above: Excitement and thrill lie in anticipation of the act as much as in the act itself.

Below: With correct training and commitment, all skiers can make their dreams come true.

THE POWDER

Let us start our skiing adventure with the best snow of all – the powder. First, however, I must emphasise my assumption that you will read the next chapter before actually going out onto the slopes and that you will use the information therein to choose a safe slope. As with learning to cruise with style, finding the best terrain is of paramount importance.

Terrain

Ideally you want a slope that is of intermediate steepness. The texture of the snow is also important, and without wanting to appear pessimistic I should say that good powder, the stuff you see in all the brochures, magazines and films, is not as easily come across as you may first think; however, soft snow can often be found and is still great fun. Pick some snow up in your hand and try to make a snowball. If it is of the right consistency, the snowball will keep breaking up and you will be able to blow it away with a strong puff. If the snow does form into a good ball, however, or if the surface of the snow is crusty, it would be best to wait for another day when conditions are more conducive to learning.

As you look down your chosen slope you should feel happy about skiing straight down it with no turns, and in fact this is just what I want you to do.

Technique

As you are sliding through the snow experiment with your fore and aft balance by rocking gently to and fro; observe your skis at the same time. You will probably find that the best position is a central one, with pressure along the length of both feet, just as you felt on the groomed slopes. There is absolutely no need to lean back, which is one of the most prevalent myths of powder skiing. Initially you may find your skis wandering slightly. Do not clamp them together as this will inhibit your progress later on. It only takes practice to be able to balance over both of them in a normal stance.

On the next run start by skiing straight down. When you are comfortable, thrust your feet down into the snow and feel the pressure build up on your heels. (You do not need to lean back to do this.) The action should be short and sharp and will create a platform from which you will feel yourself rebound upwards. Straighten you legs as you feel this rebound and allow yourself to float in the high position in which you now find yourself. As you sink again allow your legs to bend and then thrust downwards as before. You will soon feel a rhythm developing and be bouncing up and down through the powder. (A pole plant which coincides with the formation of the platform helps maintain the rhythm and should be added before you try the next stage.)

When you are happy with this bouncing movement it will be time to try some small turns, and *small* is the important word here. Get into your bouncing rhythm, then as you sink turn your feet and roll both knees very slightly, so that as the pressure builds up under your feet you feel it doing so under the inside of one foot and the outside of the other. Plant your pole, bounce up again and turn to the other side. Remember the knees should not be twisting as you roll them. You may feel as though you are turning only a little but when you get to the bottom, look back at your tracks and you will probably be surprised at just how much you were actually turning.

Coaching points

The most common error is to try to turn your feet too much. If you can handle the bouncing rhythm with no turns in the fall-line but run into trouble when you try to turn, simply reduce the turning action; it really is very little at this stage.

When you are bouncing, the up position should be held for as long as the skis float over the snow. The rhythm is 'Up, one, two, down; up, one, two, down;' and so on. Your breathing can help a great deal, so breath out forcibly as you sink and inhale as you rise.

Since your feet are only turning a

Above: For your first attempts do not try to turn too much.

small amount, your upper body remains facing straight down the slope. There should be no twisting or turning of it at this stage.

Set some realistic goals, such as completing three consecutive turns on the first run, six on the next, and so on. Look back after each run and try to see your tracks. This will give you a good indication of the radii of your turns. Judge these in the same way as you did the number of consecutive turns, three good ones on the first run, six on the next, etc. If someone has already put some tracks down that look good, try to figure eight them; that is, cross them turning the opposite way at each turn. This will help you to develop your rhythm and to judge the degree of turning required.

Below: Here the skier is figure eighting someone else's tracks to try to find the right rhythm.

The fall

Inevitably sooner or later you will fall over in the powder. The falling rarely causes problems as the landing is soft, but getting back up can use a lot of energy so I would like to offer a few hints.

As you try to get up make sure your feet are below you, as you would on the hard-pack, and then cross your poles, placing your hand on the cross as you push up. This will give you much more support if the snow is deep. When you are standing up again, dust yourself off and clear the snow from your goggles and face so that they do not

Above: Falls in powder are spectacular but rarely painful.

Below: To help yourself get up when you have fallen in soft snow, cross your poles and push off both of them.

become chilled. You may need to put your goggles inside your jacket while you sort out the rest of your gear in order to keep them from steaming up.

The chances are that you will not have been wearing leashes, so the location of your skis under all the soft snow may not be immediately obvious. It is important that you search logically because there is a

great danger of burying your skis even further by haphazard searching. The first thing to do is to recognise where you landed. Start your search at least two skis' lengths above this spot, further if you were going fast. If you have one ski, use the tail – if you have neither, use a ski pole – to cut through the snow in a diagonal grid pattern, your cuts being about a ski's width apart. Slice as deeply into the snow as possible. Continue down the slope until you find your skis. More often than not they will be close to the point where you fell. Only rarely is the snow light enough for them to

Right: To put your skis back on, first clear your boots of snow. Next, if you have any trouble proceeding as normal, place the ski you wish to put on at 90° to the one on which you are standing, resting its tail against the boot. Then step into it.

Below: To find your skis start searching about two skis' lengths above where you fell. Use a ski tail to slice through the snow in a structured pattern.

have travelled past you down the hill.

Having located your skis, clear the bindings of snow and place the downhill ski across the fall-line. Use your ski pole or the other ski to clear your boot sole of snow and step back into the ski making sure that the binding relocates firmly. Place the tail of your other ski next to the one you are standing on so

that they form an upside down T. Clear your boot sole and put the ski back on. Sometimes it will be too awkward to use this T shape, in which case put the ski on parallel to the other after making a solid platform in the snow by scraping away the loose stuff above you.

With both skis on you are ready to go again, but first remind yourself of what you were trying to do. Visualise yourself on the run and set the rhythm of your breathing, but do not fill your head with technicalities or recriminations about why you fell. If it is difficult to turn into the fall-line, dig the tails of your skis into the slope so that you can stand facing the fall-line without actually moving. Rock forwards and away you go.

Below: To start, slide the heels of your skis into the snow so you can face down the slope.

THE DEEP

Having managed a shallow slope, let us now take the technique and apply it with appropriate adaptation to steeper terrain with deeper snow. The first thing that will be obvious is that if you ski a steeper slope in the same way, you will end up going too fast, so you must add some control to your turns. You do this in much the same way as always – by turning away more from the fall-line. The basic technique is just as I have explained previously, but this time you need to exaggerate many of the movements.

Terrain

Look for a slope that is long, wide and steeper than the last one. As always, looking down the slope should fill you not with dread but excitement. You may not feel confident that you will ski it without the odd fall, but that isn't important since by now you will have discovered that falling in the powder is not too bad – chilly at times, but apart from that quite good fun! A slope that will allow you to go straight down for about 50 metres before you feel the need to slow down is ideal. The slope is unlikely to be totally untouched by other skiers, so try to find a line with the least interference from other tracks. Hitting another track is not the end of the world but may initially interrupt your rhythm so is best avoided.

Technique

Dig your heels into the snow so that you can face down the fall-line and compose yourself. You are going to use just the same movements as before: sink down and thrust your heels into the snow, plant your pole and extend with the rebound towards the fall-line, rotate your feet and roll your knees as you sink again. Your upper body is going to remain facing down the slope, meaning a degree of dynamic anticipation will be involved. This will become increasingly important as you tackle steeper slopes.

Standing there, run this sequence through your mind's eye as a visual and kinaesthetic sensation, matching your breathing with the move-

ments. Actually start the up and down rhythm while you are standing, then as you go sink down and create the platform, rebound from it and rise into the first turn. As before you will probably not need to turn as much as you first think.

Coaching points

In deep snow you still need to edge the skis, contrary to another popular myth. The difference is that the pressures under your feet are not the same as before, although the action of your legs is. You will not feel the pressure under the side of just the outside foot, rather spread over the whole sole of both feet. As you create the platform the pressure will move towards the rear of your feet. Distributing the pressure under both feet takes some practice but do not be tempted to clamp your feet together to achieve this, as that will severely hamper your progress even though it may bring success at this early stage. Persevere with independent leg action – you will soon master it.

From the turns with which you experimented in the last chapter you should be aware of your knees and hips and of the way in which concentrating on one or the other affects your turns. I now want you to experiment again in this area. Up until now you have concentrated on rolling your knees as you turn your feet, which has resulted in a fairly shallow-radius turn, unless you have been able to do it very dynamically. This time as you rise from the rebound drop your hips towards the inside of the turn and steer a wider arc. (I am assuming that by this stage of your skiing you are well able to steer the skis. If not, return to the prepared slopes and practise this first.) This action is a combination of the hip cross-over and leg extension.

A small action that may help you is to raise your outside hand as you start. This helps commit you to the cross-over phase. Do not become reliant on it, however, as it can introduce complications. It is better to concentrate on extending **up** and **into** the turn. Lifting your hand will take you towards what is known as banking.

Banking

Banking is the type of turning that was used in the powder for many years before modern equipment negated its need. Having said that, it can still be an enjoyable way of skiing deep snow and can therefore be part of your repertoire. To bank your turns you simply exaggerate the hand lifting so that it tilts your whole body, banking it into the turn. It really is as simple as that, which is perhaps one of the reasons it was so popular. However, it is a limiting technique in that it is an end in its own right, and I would like to lead you on quickly into the realms of real advanced powder skiing.

Above: Banking. Alex leans his body into the turn to edge his skis.

Adding power

As you become more comfortable with extension turns you must steadily add more power to them, as this will help when you have to tackle more difficult snow conditions. You achieve this in much the same way as you did in 'Cruising with Style'. Make good use of dynamic anticipation but this time thrust both legs forwards during the turn, especially the latter part. Clearly you must retain the extension method of initiating these turns because to use the stepping action you used on the groomed slopes would be far more difficult here. I have seen skiers ski the powder using the stepping initiation but they were all powerful racers, and generally it is not the most satisfactory technique.

UP-MOTION TURNS IN POWDER

From a low position (1), plant your pole and extend both legs (2), floating to the surface on the rebound. Lifting the outside hand (2) may help you to commit yourself to the turn (3). It is important not to turn your skis too much (4) and to maintain an even pressure under both feet.

Below: Notice how much the skier has straightened his legs. This helps the skis rise to the surface.

Right: In this heavy powder Alex has exaggerated the lifting of his outside arm to help commit himself to the turn.

KNEE CROSS-OVERS

The turn I have been describing is the classical way of skiing powder, and while it is very efficient there are many other options. In fact it could almost be said that the powder can be skied in just the same way as you ski a groomed slope, so let's experiment again.

Terrain

First we are going to try knee cross-over turns, and in the right conditions these can be real fun. It is the angle of the slope which is most critical rather than the texture of the snow, although the softer and lighter the snow the better. For your first attempt find a slope which you would be happy to schuss straight down.

Technique

Start down the fall-line and when you have reached a reasonable speed, cross your knees from one side to the other just as you did on the groomed slopes. You may experience several sensations, depending upon your speed and the degree of your crossing-over action. The first thing you may notice is that your skis sometimes remain submerged; do not worry, they are still turning as your tracks show and provided they have not caused you to pitch over the front of them it does not matter. In fact this can be a very useful experience because many skiers become obsessed with the idea that they must be able to see their skis, or at least their tips, and as a result end up sitting back in order to achieve this. With the modern softer skis you are unlikely to bury the tips so much that they become a problem, so do not be tempted to lean back unless the snow is very heavy. I will deal with such conditions later.

The next sensation you may experience as you experiment with these turns is that you are going quite fast and that there is little actual braking – hence the need to choose an appropriate slope! Because there is little or no braking the turns do feel very smooth. Try playing with the rhythm; you will find that you can alter the tempo almost at will, throwing in a few extra waggles every now and again (which do not serve much use but are fun).

Coaching points

As before these turns do need some practice because your balance is critical and your body has to learn how to react to the rapid tempo. I could describe them in more technical detail but at the end of the day it would not help. You just have to go out and keep trying them. If you find the skis are digging in and not turning enough, alter your stance so your ankles are closer to 90° with your feet and you feel the pressure under your feet closer to your heels, but not so much that your boots dig into the backs of your legs. You will know when you get it right because of the great sensation of the skis snaking beneath you. To begin with you may experience this only on a couple of turns in a run but with more miles you will be able to turn it on at will.

Above and below: Knee cross-overs in the powder.

HIP CROSS-OVERS

Hip cross-over turns can also lead to new sensations in the powder. Again you will notice the smoothness owing to the lack of braking. The radii of your turns will be much wider and you should begin to look at the terrain in a slightly different manner. Up until now we have been looking at the slope as a narrow corridor of smooth snow down the fall-line, and you have been leaving behind a trail of rhythmical, linked tracks, but I would like you to look afresh at your surroundings by combining hip rolling with banking. Notice all the small banks and hollows and think about long, smooth arcs which use the terrain to control your speed. This is how the mono-skier and snowsurfer ski, and there is no reason why you should not ski in this way on two skis. It is really up to your imagination.

Terrain
Start by using the same slope as you did for the knee cross-over turns, then later look for a slope with more interesting features on which to play with this new perception of the lines you can take.

Technique
As before head down the fall-line, pick up speed, then cross your hips over to one side. Be sensitive to the pressure under your feet and try to keep it fairly constant. Rhythm is vital, and so is commitment. If you hesitate about crossing over from one turn to the next, all will be lost. A strong pole plant will help to trigger your actions. Because of the lack of bouncing there is almost a quiet feeling to these turns, which should be cultivated and enjoyed.

Coaching points
If you find it difficult to go from one turn to the next, or the turns just do not seem to be happening, increase your speed. These turns rely for success on your having enough speed.
   Try hard to avoid bouncing; it will not hinder your ability to turn if you do bounce, it is just unnecessary and you will be missing out on one of the joys of these turns.

Speed control
I have mentioned several times how both hip and knee cross-over turns are fast and relatively free of the kind of braking felt in the leg-extension turns we looked at first. The reason is that there is an extra dimension to powder skiing, in that when you bounce up and down, there is a braking effect caused by the skis being forced deeper into the snow-pack as well as around the turn, something rarely felt as much on the groomed slopes.

Clearly without this effect speed control will be a problem on the steeper slopes with these two types of turn. A degree of braking does occur as with any turn, but sooner or later it will prove for most to be insufficient. However, it is possible to adapt these techniques to steeper ground.

Below left and below: Hip cross-overs in powder. The radii differ from those of knee cross-overs.

Below: Look at the beautiful arcs created by this skier. You do not always have to ski in a rhythm of regular turns; use your imagination and exploit the terrain to the best advantage.

COMPRESSION TURNS

The compression turn is one of the most useful turns for the skier who likes to ski snow in its natural, ungroomed state. It is a very powerful form of skiing which has been adopted by the majority of advanced powder skiers, and as such should certainly be part of your repertoire. If you have done a lot of bump skiing, you will adapt to it very quickly; if not, it will take a little longer. You can tackle the compression turn from two different angles, first on the basis of the knee cross-over turn we have been practising, and second on the basis of the traditional leg-extension turn.

Terrain
Find a slope slightly steeper than the one on which you tried knee cross-over turns.

Technique
Start with some knee cross-over turns. As you go faster and your skis shoot to the surface, let them glide over it by retracting your legs as you cross your knees over into the next turn; then thrust your skis deeper into the snow again by extending your legs. There will be some rebound from this action, which should be accompanied by a pole plant, but rather than allowing your whole body to rise up, pull your feet up towards you as though you are absorbing a bump. The skis will again be gliding over the surface with your legs bent.

Next, try the turn with the traditional powder technique. Go into your first turn and as you steer the skis away from the fall-line and extend your legs to create a platform, absorb the rebound as though it were a bump. Keep the skis on the surface by flexing your legs and keeping your body at the same level throughout.

Coaching points
Compression turns do cause you to ski faster but only up to a point. You can control your speed by steering the skis away from the fall-line more, but as you do so ensure you are ready to pole plant, as this will help your dynamic anticipation.

Be aware of your stomach muscles tightening as you pull your knees up towards you.

There may come a point at which the skis are almost uncontrollable in the sense that despite a lot of flexion in your legs they are still shooting out from the snow. If this does happen, try to ski with your ankles closer to 90° to your feet so that you can control the edges more subtly. As your skis come to the surface, push your knees to the outside of the turn and allow the edges to flatten. You will be able to rotate the skis easily from this position, and because there will be less rebound from a strongly edged ski you will feel more able to control the turn. You have come across this slightly odd position a couple of times before, especially when you were skiing the bumps, and there are times when it can prove most useful.

Below: Liz has allowed her skis to float to the surface by retracting her legs. Sometimes this action has to be performed quite positively.

COMPRESSION TURNS IN POWDER

1

As you feel yourself rebounding from the previous turn . . .

In the photograph sequence, as the skier sinks he tenses his legs so that he will rebound upwards. At that moment, instead of straightening his legs he flexes them, allowing the skis to float to the surface.

2

2

. . . allow your legs to bend.

3

Pivot your skis as they float over the surface . . .

3

. . . and extend your legs as you steer around the turn, keeping the pressure even under both feet. Your skis should be edged at this point.

4

4

SURVIVAL SKIING

Although our dreams may be full of deep powder, the reality is that sooner or later we are faced with having to cope with more difficult snows. These usually fall into two categories: heavy, sticky snow, or crud, and breakable crust. Before we look at the various tactics to adopt for coping with these, and all the variations in between, I would like to cover several survival techniques that will allow you to get out of trouble should you ever find the conditions unskiable in the normal sense of the word.

Traversing and kick turning

Very occasionally conditions can be so bad that you have to resort to traversing and kick turning. Choose your traverse line so that you can take maximum advantage of the terrain to slow down at the end of the traverse. If the terrain is of no help in this respect, you will have to step away from the fall-line until you stop. Do so with small positive steps, lifting the toe of your ski clear of the snow each time. If you are in the lead in deep crud and others plan to follow your line, you must traverse at an angle that requires you to push with your poles, otherwise those following will end up going too fast.

There are two ways in which to kick turn – facing towards and away from the slope. In this particular situation it would be usual to face away from the slope. You should practise both to ensure that you are able to perform either at will. See the photograph sequences on this and the facing page.

The three-picture sequence to the right, starting at the top, illustrates how to kick turn facing away from the slope. First, create a level platform and place your poles behind you for support (1). Then place the tail of your downhill ski next to the tip of your uphill ski (2). Allow the downhill ski to fall round in the new direction and step the uphill ski round, bringing the pole with you (3).

1

2

3

1

2

**Above left, above and below: Kick
turns facing towards the slope.
Stand on the slope as steeply as
possible (1). (The skier in these
photographs is using skins, which
give added grip on steeper slopes.)
Bring your top ski round as far as
possible, using your poles for
support (2). Step onto the ski in
the new direction (3).**

1000-step turns

This technique is a good one to
practise as it promotes independent leg action and encourages a
dynamic posture as well as being
one of the best survival techniques
I have come across.

Start on a traverse and control
your speed by stepping up the
slope away from the fall-line. As
your speed decreases, start to step
around the turn with a succession
of steps. In most conditions I find it
best to lift the toe of each ski as I
step. Continue stepping round the
turn until your speed decreases
again. Although this technique is
simple you do need to practise to
be able to perform it when it
counts.

When you are faced with impossible breakable crust, this is the
technique to try. You may have to
positively kick the toe of the ski
clear of the crust at every step and
you will need a fair degree of commitment, but it will work.

Left: 1000-step turn in the crust.

3

Stem turns

There are many variations of this basic turn and all have their role to play. It is not the turn that you came across when you were learning to ski although it will seem similar and is therefore easy to learn.

Terrain

It is always best to experiment with a technique on ground with which you can cope and, therefore, on which you can concentrate. Choose an appropriate slope.

Technique

Start with a slow traverse and when you want to turn, you have a choice. If you are uncertain of the snow, you can stem the downhill ski to test it, or if you want to turn into the fall-line as quickly as possible, you can stem the uphill ski. (It is also possible to stem both at the same time.) This movement can be made with a low body posture, which helps balance, or with an up motion, which makes the turn more flowing and thus faster. Once in the stem position steer the skis around the turn by pressuring the outside ski and steering it strongly with your leg. Stay in the stem until you are ready to traverse once again. A pole plant at this time will help to balance you as you bring the skis back to parallel.

The advantage of this turn is that it is powerful and can be done at a slow speed. It also creates a wide track behind you, which a weaker member of your party can follow if necessary.

Coaching points

Any twisting of the knees should be avoided as this can lead to injury. You are most likely to feel it, and to be most at risk, when you are in too much of a hurry to get around the turn. In most conditions you should stand over the centre of the ski you are stemming and avoid leaning back unless the tip of the ski is getting caught under the snow in such a way that it is preventing you from turning.

This is a survival technique which can still be hard work. Considerable muscular effort may be required to cut a track through the difficult snow. The faster you can go, the less muscular effort demanded of you.

Below: The skier in front has created a track for the skier behind to follow.

STEM TURNS IN THE CRUST

Up-motion turns

A solid up-motion turn can be very useful when conditions are bad, especially when linked with a degree of rotation. You will notice that I use the term 'up-motion' rather than something perhaps more familiar like 'up-unweighting'. This is because I believe that although some up-unweighting may occur, it is really the upward motion caused by extending the legs which is most significant.

Technique

The first thing that needs to be said is that for your legs to extend they need to be bent to start with, and secondly it is much easier to extend them if you are doing so from a firm platform. Finishing your turns with a strong platform is essential.

As you extend do so fully, straightening your legs as much as possible and extending not straight up but in the direction of the new turn. This last movement involves two things – a slight twisting of the upper body and a commitment to projecting yourself down the slope. This is not unlike the power turn we have

UP-MOTION TURNS

In the photographs, Alex is using a strong extension, projecting himself in the direction of the new turn, then sinking to steer around the turn.

A basic but extremely useful technique. Finish each turn strongly (1) before extending up (2, 3) and into the new turn (4). From this upright position you can sink (5) and steer powerfully around the turn (6).

looked at previously, though it does not require the same degree of wind-up and is generally a slower turn. Having extended, hold the up position until you feel yourself flowing down the slope. Just how long you should hold this position is dependent on how sharp you want the turn to be; the quicker the action the tighter the turn.

The use of the pole plant may help the turn and should be used as a trigger to the action. As your pole tip touches the snow it's as though it has thrown a switch and you immediately respond by extending: **plant** and **up**.

Clearly if you extend strongly, you will actually jump, and indeed this should be part of your repertoire,

so there is much here for you to practise.

Coaching points
First play with the extension and twisting action. As you extend concentrate on the pressure on the sole of your foot, and extend until you feel as though all the pressure is on the ball of your foot. Now concentrate on the top of your foot or instep; again, extend to varying degrees and even label the pressure as you did against your shinbone when you were experimenting with turn control. Next, be aware what the muscles in your legs are doing as you extend, particularly those at the back. The more you extend the more you will feel the tops of your calf muscles tighten.

The amount you need to twist during the extension will depend upon the snow and the terrain. You can direct the twist with your head by looking in the new direction, but the strongest sensations will come from other parts of your body, such as your shoulders, stomach muscles and hips. Concentrate on each in turn and find which gives you the best results.

If you experience difficulty with this turn, first examine the extension and then look at the twisting action. If, after experimenting with these, you feel no improvement, you must look again at the finishes of your turns and the creation of the platform, as this is where most faults occur.

Jump turns
As I mentioned earlier, a strong extension will actually lead to a jump, so let's pursue this for a moment or two. Again, the finishing of the previous turn with a solid platform is vital. There are two ways in which you can jump – with an extension as we have seen but also with a rapid retraction. The latter is a much faster action, which is

achieved by pulling your legs up quickly. Both have their place but for the moment I would like you to play around with just the extension jump.

By following your previous actions but with more vigour, your feet are certain to leave the ground and a jump turn will result. You can add several variations, however, by jumping the tails of the skis, the

whole ski or the front of the ski. All have their use so practise all of them. Any problems you experience will almost certainly be the result of an insubstantial platform.

Above: Jumping with a strong extension. The extended position allows a soft landing; hence the skis do not dig in and prevent completion of the turn.

JUMP TURNS

A sound finish to the previous turn is essential (1) and is followed by a strong extension of the legs (2). Land as softly as you can on the new edges with an emphasis on the new outside ski (3).

Windscreen-wiper turns

With these, as their name suggests, you pivot about the tails of your skis with a windscreen wiper-like motion. They are extremely useful in bad snow, especially if the slope is steep. There are two approaches. The first is to do a compression turn and then, when you want to change direction, to thrust your feet forwards and upwards so that you are on the tails of your skis. In this position pivot about your heels.

The alternative is to jump the tips of your skis around while leaning on the tails. Both approaches are fairly athletic but may prove useful on occasion.

Whatever the turn you decide to try when conditions are this bad, let go of any style and feel pleased with yourself if all you do is get down in one piece. The ability to jump back after a fall and to get on with the task of descending is what is most important. In such conditions your enjoyment usually comes just from being out there, or perhaps afterwards, when you can look back knowing you *were* out there!

Below: Windscreen-wiper turns are particularly effective in heavy snow on a steep slope.

DIFFICULT SNOWS

Having looked at survival techniques let us now see what other options we may have when encountering difficult conditions. I will start with probably the most difficult of snows – the crust.

Crust

Crust is formed either by the freeze–thaw action of the sun and frost or by the wind, so you should, by recalling the most recent weather, be able to assess how likely you are to encounter it. Even the most adventurous skiers will avoid crust if possible.

The first assessment with which you are faced on coming across crust is whether it breaks consistently or just now and again. In the case of the former, life is a little easier than in the case of the latter. Let's take the most difficult situation first.

Most people find that the compression turn works best because it allows you to be very sensitive to what is happening under your feet and yet is still a very powerful way of turning. I say 'most people' because at this level of performance you will always find skiers who, because of their strength and balance, are able to ski anything in any way.

Adopt a low stable position over your skis and focus on the pressure under your feet. The more sensitive they are to the changing state of the snow's surface, the more chance you have of reacting to it. Your turns should be gradual and of a medium radius to prevent any sudden movements which might cause the surface to break. Try to keep the pressure evenly distributed between both skis. To achieve this ski with your ankles at 90° to your feet, which, as we have seen previously, allows you to control your edges with greater subtlety. The more you edge the skis, the more chance there is of them breaking through the crust. A variation that can work in some condi-

4

COMPRESSION TURNS IN CRUST

At the end of a turn, pull your skis to the surface.

Let them float over the surface of the snow . . .

. . . and pivot them slowly. Too much turning will make them dig in.

As they sink in again, extend your legs so the skis break through under your control, and keep the pressure under both feet as even as possible.

In the photographs, the skis are trapped by the crust (top), pulled to the surface by leg retraction and turned (middle), then extended back through the crust (bottom).

tions is to use the hip cross-over in a low stance. It is the rhythm and commitment to going from one turn to the next that is important here. There must be no hesitation between turns.

With experience you will begin to notice subtle changes in the way the surface of the snow reflects light, slight variations in its colouration. These changes often indicate areas which will support you and areas where the crust will break, so use them to your advantage.

When you think the crust will support you, it will be necessary to ski very sensitively and quietly. The best technique is foot lifting with no extension. It allows you to change edges and the pressure on them with the minimum of fuss, although it does require you to ski on one ski, which may be a disadvantage if the surface only just supports you.

If the crust is breaking fairly consistently, there are a number of options open to you. Compression turns work as before but now you have to extend your legs forcibly on each turn to ensure you break through the crust.

Another alternative is the simple jump turn, which can work quite well if the crust is not too thick. The steering action needs to be powerful and the jump sufficient to clear the surface of the snow. When you land, it may be necessary to extend strongly to break through. On steeper ground the windscreen-wiper turn can be useful.

Finally, if you have ever used a monoski, you will have noticed that it is easier to use in difficult conditions. You can adapt your two-ski technique to copy the mono by skiing with your legs tight together and on the uphill or inside edge. With a fair degree of commitment this can work.

No matter which technique you try, commitment is the key word. The faster you ski and the more you commit yourself to going from one turn to the next, the more chance you will have of skiing the crust successfully.

3

Left: Clear of the snow, the skier is in a position to break through the crust with a strong extension as he lands.

JUMP TURNS IN CRUST

1

2

3

4

5

6

Either jump clear of the surface or just enough to float over it.

Experience will help you decide whether or not to break through on landing.

Powerful steering is required to drive around the turn. The faster you are prepared to go, the easier the turn becomes.

Above: The mono turn. I am standing over the inside edge of the inside ski, the same as you use the uphill edge of a monoski. The balance is critical.

Heavy, sticky snows

The next most difficult snows are the heavy, wet and sticky snows. This category covers a whole host of conditions but I want to concentrate on the very worst, those which in all likelihood are going to cause you the most problems.

Again, the compression turn will work because of the power you are able to exert through it. Avoid too much edging as this will cause the skis to throw you about. The adaptation to the basic compression turn with straighter ankles that you have used before will work well. Also, if conditions are not too sticky, the hip cross-over turn will work, providing you can maintain your speed.

The only other alternative is to make sure that your skis are clear of the snow each time you turn. This means resorting to the good old jump turn. You should strive to be as sensitive as possible on landing to prevent your skis from sinking in too far. A strong steering action is then required to complete the turn. Use the terrain to maximum advantage by looking for small launch pads in the form of bumps from which to jump.

Conditions of this kind are compounded if you have not waxed your skis properly. More than ever, therefore, you must be prepared and make sure you have used the correct mixture.

Just occasionally you will come across snow that can only be described as having a consistency similar to that of granular sugar and which collapses completely under your weight. When it is this bad (usually late in the season), you can either traverse and kick turn or adopt the dinosaur technique of straight-lining. (Remember dinosaurs? Long-necked, small brained creatures.) The latter involves you leaning back against your boots and heading straight down the fall-line. The harder you lean back, the more the tails of your skis will dig in and hence the slower you will go – at least relatively! You may have seen films or videos of monoskiers doing this, but it can also be performed on two skis, and in all snows, if the fancy takes you.

JUMP TURNS IN HEAVY SNOW

Look for lumps to jump off (2). Make sure your skis are clear of the snow (3), then land as softly as you can so your skis do not sink in too quickly (4). Strong commitment is required to steer around the turn (5).

Above left and above: In this heavy snow Alex is forced onto his heels (but does not lean back). From this position he cannot easily jump clear, so he retracts his legs to allow the skis to float to the surface, where he can turn them.

Left: Straight-lining. A fun technique that can also have its uses when snow conditions are terrible.

Ice

Ice can form both on the prepared runs and in the wilderness. In either case it causes problems for most people. The first thing that needs saying is that unless your skis are really sharp you will, at best, merely survive. If you suspect you will encounter ice and want to be able to ski it well, sharpen your edges the night before and even carry a small stone with you to hone them during the day.

There are three secrets to coping with ice. The first I have just explained. The second is to do with the line you take, and the third is your choice of technique. The line can be vital. Rarely is a whole slope icy and if you are perceptive, you will notice softer patches. Head for these and turn or break on them. It may seem obvious advice but I am always surprised at how many skiers do not use the variety of snow texture to their advantage.

Occasionally you will see very strong skiers attacking icy sections and making their skis bite with sheer brute force. Clearly this does work but for the majority of us a gentler approach gives the best results. You need to be very sensitive to your edges – too little and they will not grip, too much and they will break away. I find that foot-lifting turns allow me to be the most sensitive, and I add a varying degree of power according to the dictates of the terrain, ever conscious that too much will cause the skis to skid and break away. It is important to balance over your skis as much as possible and to avoid any banking. To achieve this you may have to angle your body more. Try dropping your outside hand towards your boots, which will have the effect of allowing your lower legs to edge the skis while your upper body remains centred over the skis.

Crud

Crud is what remains after some kind of disturbance – snow cut up by other skiers, avalanche debris, snow rubble. Here the important thing is to be on your edges as much as possible. On your edges you are stable and will not be trip-ped up by loose blocks of snow. I tend to use jump turns with a strong steering action because I do not like to ski crud too quickly – it is too easy to be caught out by a sudden large lump of snow. The exception to this is in cut-up powder, where I use a low form of the hip cross-over turn. This forces me to maintain my rhythm while the low stance helps me to keep my balance.

When I lead ski tours, I always prefer skiers who have the ability to pick themselves up after a fall, dust themselves down and get on with their descent, to good skiers who are always worried about how they are skiing. When we hit difficult snows it is tough for everybody, and the most important thing is not to get despondent and certainly not to worry about what you look like! Treat bad conditions as a challenge and remember the more time you spend trying to ski them, the better you will get.

WHITEOUT

Now I want to deal with one further problem you will encounter – the whiteout. This occurs when the light is so bad that you cannot distinguish any horizon. Because usually we rely so heavily on our sense of sight for feedback about our surroundings and what is happening within them, it is easy to become totally disorientated. Understanding this leads to the obvious solution. We need to use our other senses to tell us what is happening.

Start with your feet. Feel the texture of the snow under them and develop a sense of the slope and where the fall-line lies. Use techniques that give you maximum feedback by maintaining an even pressure under your feet, such as hip cross-over turns.

Drag your poles so that they give you feedback about how fast you are moving, and feel the wind on your face caused by your forward passage.

Use turns that demand a constant rhythm and thus minimise hesitation between turns. If you are very unsure what lies ahead, use turns which have a strong check. You will lose some feedback with these because they require you to jump at their initiation, but they will allow you to control your speed. The skidding they cause will give you very good feedback about your speed.

Trees

When visibility is poor, it is a good time to head for the trees, where their shadows will help to give the terrain form and shape. If the snow cover is deep, tree-line skiing is quite safe, though it is wise to remove your hands from your wrist loops so that the poles do not wrench your shoulders if they get caught in the branches. If, on the other hand, you are uncertain of the snow's depth, there is a risk of tree roots and stumps catching you out. Under these circumstances I make sure my ski tips are showing and cannot slide under a hidden root.

Many people are daunted by the prospect of skiing through nature's slalom course. The best advice I can give you may seem glib but it is in fact very sound. Look for the gaps between the trees, not the trees themselves. Ski for these gaps and make sure you turn before them, not at them. This change of perception is the same tactic that the slalom racer uses in choosing his or her line. It is very effective.

Below: In trees it is a good idea to remove your hands from your straps. Only remove your goggles for short periods of time, even if it is cloudy, and replace them when the trees are dense to protect your eyes from branches.

THE STEEP

The steep really comes in two categories:

1. Steeper ground than you would normally find on the prepared runs which, although frightening, is no more dangerous than a steep bump field.

2. Super steep ground where the penalties for a mistake are very high indeed. This is often known as 'ski extreme'.

Let us start with the first of these.

To ski steep ground you need to use a family of turns known as short swings, which are short-radius turns with a strong check. You can group these quite neatly according to the way in which you jump and the point about which your skis rotate. First you must find an appropriate slope.

Terrain

Find a slope with a gradient of about 35°, preferably covered in reasonably soft snow. It does not need to be very long, a stretch of 20 metres being quite adequate for your first attempts. The slope should feel steep but not terrifying.

A certain adrenalin buzz will do no harm but you do not want to be quaking in your boots!

Technique

In the jump turns we dealt with earlier, you left the ground by extending your legs. There is an alternative, and that is to retract your legs quickly – a much quicker action. Whichever way you jump, you need a good platform from which to take off, and this you create by steering the skis powerfully around the turn, then moving your thighs sharply in towards the slope as a checking

SHORT SWINGS WITH EXTENSION

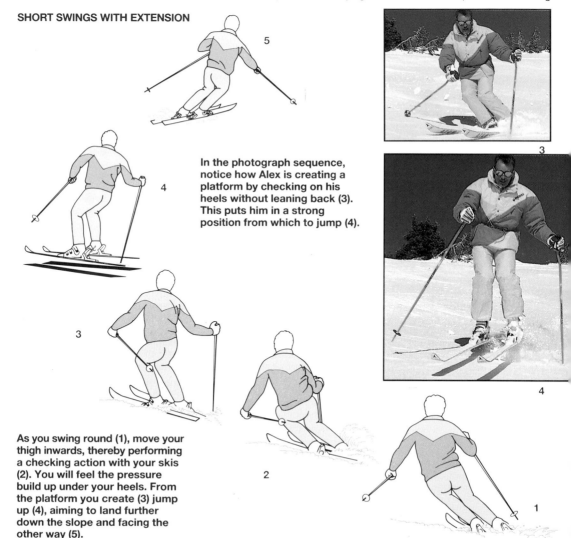

In the photograph sequence, notice how Alex is creating a platform by checking on his heels without leaning back (3). This puts him in a strong position from which to jump (4).

As you swing round (1), move your thigh inwards, thereby performing a checking action with your skis (2). You will feel the pressure build up under your heels. From the platform you create (3) jump up (4), aiming to land further down the slope and facing the other way (5).

action. From this you will get a rebound and a positive jump. The check should coincide with a pole plant.

For your first turns I suggest you start with leg extension jumps and rotate around a point halfway between the tips of your skis and your feet. Providing the slope is not too narrow this will remain one of the most effective techniques.

Start in a steep traverse and as your speed picks up steer the skis in an arc away from the fall-line. As you begin to slow down check hard by moving you thighs inwards, pole plant down the slope and jump the skis around to a point just beyond the fall-line. You should feel the pressure from the checking action under your heels. As you land do so softly and let the skis skid around until you are repeating the manoeuvre in the other direction.

Coaching points

What I have described here is a defensive style of skiing. As you become more proficient, try to turn it into a more offensive style by taking charge of your skis earlier in the turn. Pivot and skid them less and use your power to steer them around. Ultimately this will lead to greater control and a more efficient harnessing of your effort. This applies also to the variations I am about to describe.

If your feet are close together on steep ground, they will really inhibit your actions, so be sure they are well apart.

As you jump, aim to land not only on the other side of the fall-line but also slightly downhill. Initially you will probably land some distance from the fall-line and end up skidding a lot, but as you become more proficient so you will find yourself landing closer to the fall-line and steering your skis around the turn more positively.

A solid pole plant is essential – start reaching down the slope for it as soon as your skis begin to turn. This action will help to commit you to the next turn, angle the edges on your skis more and force you to anticipate the turn.

Use your breathing to help with the rhythm; your voice can also be used to good effect. Rhythm is very important, especially on long slopes; without it you will soon become tired.

In the same way that increasing your speed on shallower slopes leads eventually to more control, so skiing steeper and steeper slopes improves your control when you return to shallower slopes.

Short swings with leg retraction

You need to change to this technique when the slopes become steeper and narrower.

Above and below: Short swings with leg retraction. Reaching down the slope for the pole plant.

Terrain
Use the slope you have been practising on so far in this section– steep, but not too steep.
Technique
Start the first turn in exactly the same way but jump with a leg-retracting action and pivot the skis about your feet. Land on both feet and be ready to pole plant almost straightaway.

Because you are pivoting the skis about your feet, you should find that you turn almost 180° with the jump. The timing of your pole plant will vary. Sometimes it is useful to plant it as you land in order to give yourself a third point of stability, but this technique can cause problems if you then skid onto the pole. When the snow is suspect, prod it with the pole until it feels right to turn.
Coaching points
The amount you skid and the amount you actually pivot the skis will depend upon the steepness of the slope, how narrow it is, the condition of the snow and your mental state. There will be occasions, such as when you are skiing steep breakable crust, when you will literally be jumping down the slope in a series of leaps from one set of edges to the other. When the slope is covered with spring snow, the sun is shining and you are feeling great, you will be able to take the jarring out of these turns and ski rhythmical short turns all the way down.

Windscreen-wiper technique
The final method entails pivoting about the tails of your skis and is useful in very bad snow on a steep slope. Sylvan Saudan, one of the original skiers of the extreme, made this technique his own. As we have seen, it is quite a good way of coping with heavy snow, and the technique of using it on the steep is more or less the same as you have already learnt. As you steer round the turn thrust your feet forward, pole plant and then, leaning on the pole, pivot the tips of your skis around. On steeper terrain you will need to jump the tips around as it will be more difficult to lean on your pole.

All of these techniques will be fine on any gradient up to about 45°, but when it gets really steep you will have to make another adaptation. In the 50° region it becomes very difficult to jump off the lower leg and you will need to jump off the uphill edge of the top ski by extending that leg. When you are in the air, retract your legs by tucking your heels below you, which allows the skis past the snow behind. You will have to land on both skis and be sure to be reaching down the slope with your pole ready for the next turn. On this type of slope it is unlikely that your turns will have any rhythm – each will be a separate entity. There will be a lot of skidding as you test the snow prior to each turn.

Extreme skiing is dangerous – a mistake could easily cost you your life. You need to be fit and technically sound; most of all, you must want to be there for the right reasons. If you are not sure what the right reasons are, perhaps you should not be taking your skiing in this direction.

Above and right: Ski extreme. On steep ground it may be necessary to take off from the inside ski because the downhill, or outside, leg is so straight.

SKINNING

In the past adventure skiing was of two distinct kinds: off-piste skiing (as it is known in Europe), which uses the uphill transport of the resort, and ski-touring or ski-mountaineering, which relies entirely on your own energy. Ski-touring is great fun but you have to have the mentality, not to mention the knowledge, of the mountaineer and to enjoy climbing uphill. Off-piste skiing, on the other-hand, severely limits the terrain you can reach. However, it is now possible with slight adaptations of equipment to blend the two extremes together. With the use of a touring binding, or a fitting to adapt a normal binding, and a pair of skins it is possible to reach slopes that hitherto would have involved excessive effort for the skier. Half an hour's climbing can open up a whole new vista of slopes. Before we get carried away, however, there is a price to be paid, and that is the increased danger. You must, as with any adventure

skiing, be prepared to take responsibility for your actions, and you can only do this if you are fully informed as to what you are letting yourself in for. For this reason I urge you again to read the next chapter in conjunction with this one.

Whether you are using touring bindings or an adaptation of your downhill bindings, the technique for using skins remains the same. Rear-entry boots are best because they allow you to walk more easily when they are undone. If you have front entry boots, be sure to loosen the cuff clips otherwise you will bruise your shin bones. It is almost universally accepted that stick-on skins are the best. These are covered with a glue that does not dry and which sticks to a dry ski base. Many have a hooking system as well, and I certainly favour the extra security this offers. The skins must be kept dry and preferably warm if you are to gain the maximum benefit from the glue.

Walking on skins only requires practice, and if you are faced with a long section involving little climbing, rub some wax into the skin to allow it to glide more easily. When you start climbing uphill, make sure you keep the pressure centred over the ski. If you edge the ski at all, it will slide because the edge is not covered by the skin; and if you push too much off the toes as you move forwards again, the skin will not grip. Most of the time you will ascend in a series of zig-zags linked by kick turns. Your uphill hand will always be higher so hold the pole at half height to alleviate any aching. Unless it is very steep or the snow is deep you will usually find it easier to kick turn facing towards the slope. Make sure you are well practised before trying to climb up a long slope.

Touring techniques can open up a whole new world but one that is really beyond the scope of this book. If you feel it is a world you would like to explore, the final section in Chapter 7, on ski mountaineering, might whet your appetite a little more. However, I suggest you read much further and even consider getting some specialised instruction because there is a great deal to learn.

Above: Applying the skins to the ski bases.

Below: A Secura-fix climbing device that can be used with normal downhill equipment.

Far left and left: Sometimes a short walk is worth the effort.

CHAPTER 5

MOUNTAIN LORE

Watching snow fall I always marvel at how such a delicate thing as a snowflake can shape our world. Not only does it provide the medium for one of humankind's most exciting sports, but it shapes the very environment in which we enjoy that sport. The snowflake consolidates ultimately into the glacier and that, in turn, carves the mountain architecture that leaves so few of us who see it unmoved. It is hard to imagine that the great rock walls of Yosemite or the great north faces of the Alps are, at least in part, the result of the delicate snowflake. This process, of course, takes a very long time but the power of the snowflake can be seen in the much more immediate and violent form of the avalanche.

Avalanches are not something that just happens to other people. The more time you spend skiing away from the prepared tracks, the greater the chance of your being involved in an avalanche either as a victim or as a potential rescuer. The knowledge available that will reduce the odds of your being caught and improve your effectiveness as a rescuer is not difficult to assimilate. It also has the added benefit of increasing your understanding of the environment, and this in turn will help you to find better conditions in which to ski.

It is unwise to think of avalanches totally in terms of hard and fast rules. There are so many variables that although some slopes are more prone than others, there is always the exception and that might be the slope on which you choose to ski. For this reason I think it is best to try to understand the principles of snow-pack instability so that you can approach each slope independently and equipped with a list of practical checks to carry out.

RESORT ASSESSMENT

Your assessment of conditions can start on arrival at your ski area. Consult other skiers and in particular the locals. They may be able to tell you if any slopes are particularly prone to avalanches. Clearly you have to be selective about whom you take advice from. Qualified guides and the ski patrollers are probably the most reliable sources but they are often hard to find.

You also need to have some idea about what the recent weather has been like. The most dangerous time for avalanches is during a storm and for about 24 hours afterwards, as the snow-pack needs time to settle. This frequently presents something of a dilemma because as soon as a storm abates the best powder always seems to get skied. Just because a slope has already been skied, however, is no guarantee that it is stable. In many ski areas there are avalanche assessment boards which grade the level of instability. All resorts indicate whether or not the risk is high but unfortunately some do not remove the avalanche signal even when the risk has gone, which means people lose faith in them. Even so it would be wise to heed their warnings and perhaps find out what their policy is regarding the assessment of risk. Even if they say the situation is safe they cannot assess every slope, so you must take their advice only as qualified guidance. You should still make your own on-the-spot assessments.

Having marked on your map those areas known to be unstable, it is also worth noting from which direction the last storm came, which way the wind was blowing and which way it is currently blowing. These facts will prove useful for your on-site assessment.

Top left and left: The power of the snowflake. If you ski off the groomed slopes, you should be versed in avalanche procedure.

Above: Avalanche information.

Below: An avalanche warning flag.

ON-SITE ASSESSMENT

There are basically two types of avalanche – loose snow and slab. Loose-snow avalanches occur when a fragment of snow breaks away. It can be as small as a single crystal but more typically is about the size of a snowball. This starts a chain reaction and an avalanche ensues. Loose-snow avalanches vary tremendously in size but are usually seen as small sluffs; huge ones are rare in ski resorts. Generally they do not offer a threat to the skier though even small sluffs can knock you off your feet if you are not careful. Slab avalanches, on the other hand, are very serious and must be watched out for. There are a number of simple tests you can make in order to judge whether or not a slope is stable. Let us start with the simplest, what I have called the 3 As Test.

The 3 As test

The three As stand for aspect, altitude and angle. The aspect of a slope is the direction in which it

Below: The 3 As. There are three avalanches in this picture, of similar altitude, aspect and angle.

THE 3 As

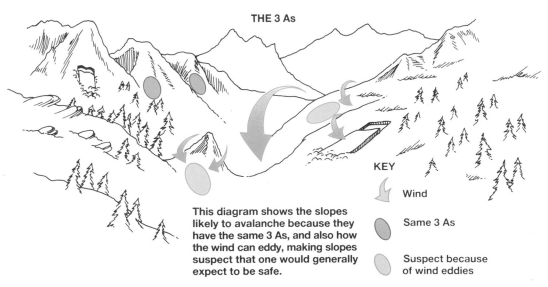

This diagram shows the slopes likely to avalanche because they have the same 3 As, and also how the wind can eddy, making slopes suspect that one would generally expect to be safe.

KEY

Wind

Same 3 As

Suspect because of wind eddies

faces, the altitude is its height above sea level, and the angle is its gradient (measured in degrees from the horizontal). The actual figures are not important; what is important, however, is that if a slope has avalanched, all slopes with the same 3 As will be suspect. You can either look around you, noting from those slopes that have already gone which are also likely to do so, or when you reach the slope you want to ski, check slopes with the same 3 As and see what has happened to them.

You should also look for obvious signs of instability. Slumping on other slopes may indicate that yours is also unstable. Cracks in the slope certainly indicate slabs that may slide, and slabs that break away from your skis as you approach a slope also indicate a weakness. Occasionally you may hear a slope settle with an ominous 'crump', which is a sign that there might be air-pockets or a weak layer beneath the top slab, a very dangerous situation. These checks give you a quick indication only and it is important always to consider the whole situation, so let us now look at some of the other factors that may influence the stability of a slope.

Below: Stress in the snow-pack has caused this crack to appear.

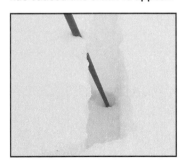

Temperature
As soon as snow falls it begins to undergo changes which are dependent on the temperature differences within the snow-pack. The most common process is known as equitemperature metamorphism, or ET met for short. It results in the breakdown and rounding off of the snowflakes and accounts for the fact that often the best powder is found some time after a fall of snow. If the process continues, these rounded particles join together again, eventually forming a strong cohesive layer (known in Europe as firn snow). The speed of this process is temperature dependent. In temperatures near to $0°$ C it is rapid, but in lower temperatures near to $-40°C$ it stops altogether. This means that the chances of loose-snow avalanches are increased when the temperature remains low for long periods.

Because snow has an insulating effect it is possible for the ground beneath to be warmer than the surface snow, resulting in a condition known as temperature gradient metamorphism, or TG met for short. TG met occurs when the air temperature is cold and the snow layer shallow and unconsolidated. Over a few days, the resulting vertical migration of water vapour causes the formation of fragile, cup-like crystals known as depth hoar. These crystals form a very weak layer within the snow-pack which can collapse, thereby releasing a slab avalanche. Layers of this kind are most commonly found on north- and east-facing slopes that receive little sun, although they have also been found on sunny south-facing slopes. If the season started with a fall of snow followed by a sustained period of cold, dry weather, you should suspect this condition and beware. Depth hoar is usually found close to the ground or next to ice and sun-crust layers within the snow-pack and is more prevalent at higher altitudes. Hoar also occurs at the surface, which in itself causes no problems but when it is buried by a fresh layer of snow, it becomes as lethal as depth hoar.

The final effect of temperature is in the melt–freeze cycle, known as MF metamorphism. This is significant in the formation of icy layers and wet layers within the pack, both of which can cause slides.

Although you may find grounds for suspecting all of these conditions by examining the recent and current weather, it is only by inspecting the snow-pack itself that you can really be sure. Before we do that, however, let us consider another climatic factor – the wind.

Above: Surface hoar.

Wind

When the wind blows it picks up snowflakes, and the stronger it blows the more it picks up. As they are blown about, the snowflakes collide with each other and the ground. Their delicate branches break off, leaving crystals which compact together very tightly. If the wind is forced by the terrain to slow down, it is no longer able to carry as much snow and dumps some or all of its load, forming what is known as wind-slab.

Wind-slab is recognisable by its milky, opaque appearance and it usually squeaks under your edges or as you rotate a pole in it. Depending on the conditions under which it is deposited, it varies in consistency from a hard slab into which your edges only just cut to a soft slab that settles under your skis.

The problem with wind-slab is that it does not adhere to snow beneath or on top of it, and all slab avalanches are the result of one layer sliding over another.

Bottom left: The cornices along this ridge are quite clear and indicate the presence of wind-slab on the slopes below.

Below: Sastrugi are formed by the action of wind scouring.

The first measure for avoiding wind-slab is to take account of the wind action. Wind slows down on the lee side of a slope, and it is here that it deposits wind-slab. What you must be very careful about is eddies caused by the terrain. These can deposit wind-slab on slopes in a completely different direction from the principal air-stream.

Wind-slab can be very localised. You will have to assess a slope taking into account every small ridge and bump which might cause the wind to change direction. There are several signs that the wind has been blowing. Sastrugi are wind-etched features in the snow that indicate from where snow has been stripped. Their general shape may indicate the direction from which the wind was blowing. Rime ice, formed from super-cooled water droplets, appears on the windward side of any obstacle.

The second measure is to examine the structure of the snow-pack by digging a pit.

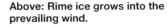

Above: Rime ice grows into the prevailing wind.

Below: Sastrugi can be small and delicate or as high as your knees.

The snow-pack

Examining the snow-pack is the best way of assessing the avalanche potential of a slope, and the only way in which you can examine the snow-pack correctly is to dig a pit. Provided you carry a shovel (which, after reading the section on avalanches, I hope you will), this is not such an onerous task. The site of the pit must be as close as possible to the slope you are assessing without actually endangering yourself and your party.

The pit should be about one and a half shovel widths wide at the back and slightly wider at the front. It should be as deep as possible, reaching down either to the bedrock or at least as far as the major stable layers. The back face and the sides should be scraped smooth so that you can see the layering clearly.

There are three factors to consider: the hardness of the layers, the size of snow crystals and the wetness of the layers. First establish what layers there are, then assess whether there are any significant differences between them. If a layer that can be penetrated only by a sharp implement lies immediately above or below one that can be penetrated by your finger, it is dangerous. You can grade the hardness of layers by using progressively blunter objects: 1. knife blade, 2. ski pole, 3. single finger, 4. four fingers, and 5. a fist. This may allow you to make a more objective assessment. The snow should be tested every couple of centimetres as some layers can be wafer thin.

Next check crystal sizes, and again it is large differences that are the warning signs. Follow this by looking at the wetness of each layer and in particular any free-running water. Wet snow within the snow-pack can be extremely serious because it acts as a lubricant over which other layers move. Finally, check the ground surface. Grass and smooth rock are particularly dangerous, especially when associated with water.

Before making your final judgement cut two diverging slots at the back of the pit, a shovel's width apart. Push your shovel between these so that it is parallel with the front edge. By pulling the shovel directly towards you, keeping the handle perpendicular to the slope,

Below: The gradient of a slope can be assessed with ski poles. If the horizontal pole bisects the vertical, the gradient is 30°. If they bisect each other, as here, the gradient is 45°. Slopes with gradients between these two angles are at most risk.

Right (top, middle, bottom): A pit revealing a suspect layer. At the back I have made two oblique cuts, isolating a pillar of snow. Placing the shovel across these, I pull perpendicularly towards me.

Below: If the unstable surface layer is only the width of your hand, you need have little worry.

you can test the cohesiveness of each layer. It is a subjective test but with experience you will be able to assess which are the layers that slide easily. Very bad layers will slide almost as you insert the shovel.

Profiles should be examined regularly, even if you think conditions are safe, because the snow-pack is always changing. The problem with digging pits everywhere is that it is time consuming. I frequently use my ski pole to check quickly whether conditions have altered. Insert the pole as deeply as you can and rotate it to make a conical hole. Repeat this several times until you can see the profile, then check if it follows the same pattern as in your last pit by probing the snow layers with the pole-tip and basket.

Finally, I ought to point out that pits themselves can be hazards to other skiers if you do not site them with care. You do not want to be halfway down a great powder run only to be confronted by a man-made hole!

By considering the factors mentioned so far you should be able to make an assessment of a slope's safeness. That assessment will lead you to one of three conclusions: either the slope is perfectly safe and you can proceed, or you are not quite sure, or it is definitely unsafe and you must find an alternative. The problem lies, of course, with the second conclusion, but there is a further check that can be made and that involves test-skiing the slope.

Below: A ski-pole test later on indicates whether or not the weak layer is still present.

Test-skiing a slope

This is really a last resort for when there is no other possible route. If you can find a slope that has the same 3 As as yours but is short and has an easy run-out, you can test it by skiing and jumping around on it. You must choose the slope carefully because this is obviously a hazardous undertaking, but you may be surprised at how many slopes lie close to the main ones you want to ski. If no such slope is to be found, however, and you have no option but to descend your chosen route, you will have to test the slope attached to a length of rope which is belayed by a partner. This is fairly drastic but it is not out of the question that you will be faced by the need to carry out such a check. If you are going to ski away from the prepared tracks, you should be as self-sufficient as possible. The techniques are not hard to learn and could get you out of a lot of trouble. The extra equipment does not amount to much and there are other occasions when it might prove useful.

There are three ways in which partners can anchor themselves:

1. They sit in the snow and dig the heels of their skis into it. The more they are wedged in the better. In this position they can use a waist belay or an Italian hitch on a sling round the skis below their boots.

2. They remove their skis and bury them in a trough at 90° to the fall-line. A sling is wrapped around the skis, which are placed sole to sole and tip to tail. An Italian hitch is operated from this sling. The skis must be buried deep enough not to pull against a weak layer themselves and a trough dug for the sling and rope to slide through. This is a very strong anchor but does take time to set up.

3. Fix the sling or a loop of rope to a spike of rock. If you use a sling, run the Italian hitch from this. If you do not have a sling, tie a figure-of-eight knot, loop it over the spike, and attach the belayer to one end of the rope, making sure he or she is tight on the anchor. They can then use a waist belay.

Once your partner is anchored, tie the end of the rope round your waist using a figure-of-eight knot that is as tight as possible (this is very important). Proceed out onto the suspect slope and try hard to make it release by jumping up and down. If it proves to be stable, you should still proceed with caution and choose the safest line.

Below: Test-skiing a slope.

WAIST BELAY

Slide the rope round your waist, . . .

. . . left hand pulling, right extending.

Slide your left hand forwards . . .

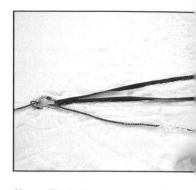

. . . and move your right hand over to your left.

Grip both sections of rope with your left hand and slide your right hand back. Repeat the sequence.

To hold a fall, move both arms in and grip.

Above: The belayer passes a sling, with a karabiner attached, round the heels of his skis, then digs his heels into the snow. He uses an Italian hitch to safeguard the skier.

Below and bottom: A buried ski anchor. The skis are placed tip to tail and a sling passed round them. They are buried in a trough with a slot to prevent them being lifted out when tension is exerted on the rope. The belayer can either attach him- or herself to this anchor and use a waist belay, or attach an Italian hitch to it.

ITALIAN HITCH

When the two bights of rope are brought together, the karabiner can be clipped round both of them. Control by the seated skier, whose skis are stuck into the snow with the sling passed round them, is weaker than control from below, but adequate.

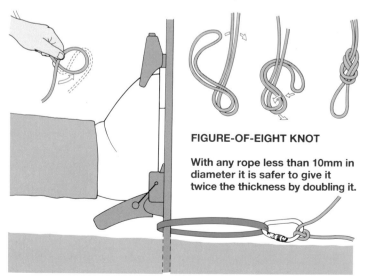

FIGURE-OF-EIGHT KNOT

With any rope less than 10mm in diameter it is safer to give it twice the thickness by doubling it.

CHOOSING A SAFE LINE

As you look at your proposed line of descent consider first the possible effects of wind action. Where will it have deposited snow and where will it have stripped it? Head for the areas where it has been stripped. These will be the ridges – even the very small ones will be better than the hollows in between. Consider next the shape of the slope. Concave slopes tend to compress the snow-pack and are therefore safer than convex slopes, which put it under tension. Use your map (I will go into greater detail about this later) to anticipate the slopes ahead. Also take into account the gradient of the slope. Most avalanches occur on slopes of between 28° and 45° from the horizontal. Tree-lined slopes are safer than others, as are uneven rocky slopes, but neither is any guarantee of safety. Finally, ask yourself what would happen if you did get caught by an avalanche. Where would it take you? Do not ski a line that would put you in danger of being swept over a cliff or into a gulley. How you and the rest of your party ski the slope is important.

Below left and below: The end of the rope has been doubled and a figure-of-eight knot tied using the double thickness to make it more comfortable. After stepping into the loop so formed, tighten it firmly around your waist.

Below: Even apparently innocuous slopes can be hazardous. It does not take long to check.

SKIING A SUSPECT SLOPE

Setting out from a safe vantage point, ski the slope individually, taking great care to watch each other continuously. Before you set off do up your clothing fully, covering your mouth and nose if possible. Spare clothing should be worn rather than carried in a pack. All of these precautions will help you survive in the event of your being buried. Take your hands out of the wrist loops of your poles and if you are wearing safety straps, undo them. When you are skiing the slope, try to remain aware of what is happening around you and keep an eye out for exit routes. If it is possible just to cross the slope, all do so by the same route, quickly and one at a time. If you are the first to traverse the slope and are breaking trail, it is worth taking care to proceed at an angle that requires you to use your poles, otherwise when the others follow they will go too fast in your tracks.

With all the knowledge and caution in the world, of course, it is still possible to be caught if you continue to ski untracked snow. I do not say this to scare you, rather to encourage you to learn as much as possible, because by doing so you will reduce considerably the chances of having an accident. What should you do, however, if you are caught?

AVALANCHES

Generally, avalanches occur with no warning. One minute you are standing on, or skiing through, wonderfully smooth snow and the next you've been caught. At this moment there are several things you can try that will increase your chances of survival. Once, while descending a mountain in the Himalayas, I skied cautiously around a corner but as soon as my skis touched the new slope it avalanched. More as a reaction than a calculated measure, I thrust my poles deeply into the solid snow beneath and jumped up the slope. The slide disappeared below me and I edged my way very gingerly back to safer ground. It was a small

avalanche and I am sure that had it been any bigger, I would have been swept down with it. The point is that you should try everything to prevent being swept away, especially since most avalanches are caused by skiers themselves.

If you are caught

In the event of your being caught there are two courses of action you can try. First, if the avalanche is not too deep, it is possible to ski out of it. I will relate an incident that happened to me in the hope that you will learn something from it.

I was skiing in Switzerland and was only a few yards from a prepared slope when an avalanche went. I turned downhill and continued to ski, going what appeared to be faster than the moving snow around me. It also felt right to keep turning. By going faster than the snow I was able to maintain a degree of control in the same way as a white water canoeist, who must either go faster or slower than the current in order to steer his craft. The action of turning seemed to help surprisingly in maintaining my balance. All the while I was desperately looking for an escape route by which I could ski out of the path of the avalanche. Once again there was little calculated thought, it was more a case of reacting to the situation as it developed. Fortunately the slope ran out naturally, and I skied away from the avalanche as it slowed down. Skiing out of an avalanche demands great skill or great luck – I lay claim only to the latter. But since to stand there passively is almost certainly going to end in disaster you might as well have a go.

The second course of action, of which I am glad to say I have not had first-hand experience, is what is classically recommended. As soon as you are swept away discard your skis, poles and sack and try either a swimming action or a rolling action in an effort to stay near the surface. For some years I was sceptical about this, in that I did not think you would have time to remove skis etc., but a few seasons ago I met a group I had been training earlier. They had had the

misfortune to have been caught by a fairly large avalanche in Les 2 Alpes in France. They had been surprised to find that they had in fact had time to remove not only their skis but also their sacks and poles, and all of them escaped without serious injury. I have also spoken to a number of avalanche victims who have used the rolling action very successfully, and this seems to be favoured over the swimming action. Whatever the action, it is imperative to stay on the surface for as long as possible, especially as the slide comes to a halt.

If you are close to the surface, you will not only sustain fewer injuries but it will be easier to locate

Below: Are you ready for the commitment this kind of terrain demands?

you. Once the snow is still, try to remain calm; you will need all your energy to stay warm, and shouting, unless you are at the surface, will go unnoticed, although a good, loud shout just before you are buried may draw attention to you, giving any potential rescuers a clue as to where to start looking. It is now time to hope that your avalanche transceiver is working correctly. You are, of course, wearing one, aren't you? If you are not, your chances of survival are very slim indeed.

Chances of survival

The statistics of the rescue services allow us to examine the probability of survival in relation to the duration and depth of burial, as depicted in the diagram on page 91. What these consistently show is that the chances of survival are severely diminished the longer you are buried and that this is especially so after the first two hours. From this it is clear that the sooner a search is instigated, the greater the chance of survival, and that this must be a major consideration when reviewing the searching devices available.

Searching devices

The simplest device on the market is a reflective plate that can be stuck to your boot; however, with this it is necessary to call out the rescue teams which have the requisite homing device, and this can take up valuable time. The plate does, however, have the advantage of being relatively inexpensive.

The only really viable answer is a device known as a transceiver. This can both transmit and receive signals, and when carried by all party members it allows any one or more of them who may be buried to be located in the shortest possible time. It is very accurate and relatively simple to use, though it does need practice. It operates on two frequencies, 457 kHz and 2275 kHz. IKAR (the International Commission for Mountain Rescue) has determined that 457 kHz is the better frequency to use, and in Europe it recommends that eventually everybody turns over to it; there are no such plans in North America, however, where 2275 kHz is favoured. Most manufacturers now produce dual-frequency models, allowing compatibility between different transceivers.

The signal strength can be adjusted and is heard via a small microphone or ear-piece. Some models feature both, and a few include a visual display as well. The transceiver must be worn underneath clothing so there is no chance of it being ripped off by an avalanche. It should be turned on at

the start of the day and its batteries checked, then tested to see if it is transmitting. Do not be selective about turning it on and off, because when confronted by a field of fresh powder you may just forget to turn it on. Better it be on all day and turned off only when you get home.

Using a transceiver

Let us now consider how to use a transceiver in the event of an ac-

Left: The ARVA 4000 is a typical transceiver, worn under clothing to prevent it being torn free.

Below: The red arrows represent the transceivers' range. At each turn of the search the volume is reduced to a minimum.

cident. Imagine you are one of a party of three. You arrive at a ridge, and the slope to the right looks great. One of your friends sets off and is avalanched. You must watch him and mentally mark where you last see him before he is buried. Look for anything that might indicate where he is – a ski pole, a ski or an item of clothing, for example. In this case you spot a ski poking through the snow just below where you last saw him. Check the slope above: it is unlikely to avalanche again because all the tension will have been taken out of the snowpack, but just in case ski over to the debris one at a time. Spread yourselves out across the avalanche so that the range of your transceivers covers the debris, then move downhill in line. It may be necessary to

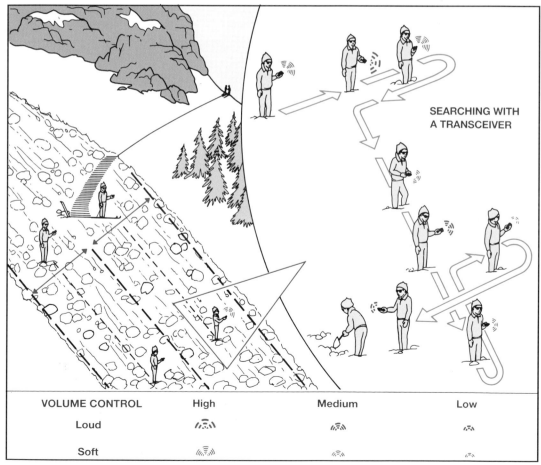

SEARCHING WITH A TRANSCEIVER

VOLUME CONTROL	High	Medium	Low
Loud			
Soft			

move down in a zig-zag fashion if it is a really wide avalanche.

When you hear a signal and there is only one person buried, concentrate on the receiving transceiver. If more are buried, care has to be taken not to confuse the different signals. Turn the volume down until you can only just hear it and rotate the transceiver through 360 degrees vertically and horizontally until you find the strongest signal. It will now be aligned with the buried one. Traverse the slope to your left. If the signal diminishes, turn 180 degrees and return to the point where it is loudest. Turn the volume down once more, then turn 90 degrees down the slope and again find the spot where the volume is loudest. Repeat the 90 degrees pattern until your transceiver is turned to the lowest volume and you have found where that is at its loudest. The victim will now be very close, so start digging.

It is possible to pin-point the other transceiver, but this can waste valuable minutes; you only need to be within about a metre of it and your digging will uncover the victim. Many models are also directional, and it is possible to use this directionality to search, but this requires more practice than the 90 degrees method.

Occasionally as you zero in on the victim's signal you may find your transceiver goes dead. If this happens, do not change direction but continue on your course until you pick up a signal again; then return to a spot halfway between the point at which you now find yourself and the point at which the signal disappeared. You should then be over the victim. This phenomenon occurs because of a particular signal configuration which relates to the depth at which the victim is buried.

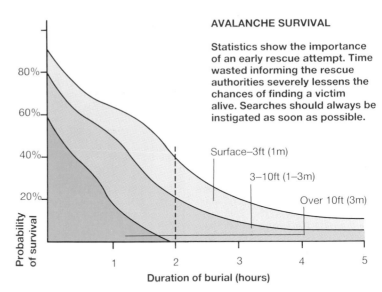

AVALANCHE SURVIVAL

Statistics show the importance of an early rescue attempt. Time wasted informing the rescue authorities severely lessens the chances of finding a victim alive. Searches should always be instigated as soon as possible.

Surface–3ft (1m)

3–10ft (1–3m)

Over 10ft (3m)

Probability of survival

Duration of burial (hours)

Below: A probe search of avalanche debris. This is a very laborious method compared with the use of transceivers, which offers far more hope. Which would you prefer to depend on?

ACCIDENT PROCEDURE

Accidents unfortunately happen to the best of us, especially when we are wilderness skiing, and although what follows may seem pessimistic, I hope it will give you confidence both about how much you can constructively do and about your true responsibilities.

When you are skiing away from the prepared slopes, you cannot and should not rely on the rescue services to bail you out. If you expect them to help, you should not ski there but remain on terrain which they serve. I am not being critical of those who ski only in patrolled areas, but I am of those who venture beyond while expecting others to help them out when things go wrong. If you notice a change in what I hope is my normal easy-going manner, it is because this is something about which I feel very strongly. You must take complete responsibility for your own actions. With this attitude of mind you will be much safer, providing you educate yourself correctly. Part of this educative process is becoming familiar with some basic first aid procedures. Do not be daunted by this prospect; it is very unlikely that you will do any harm to a victim, and not having a go is usually far worse. What I am going to deal with here is those aspects that are of particular relevance to the wilderness skier. I will not be dealing with actual diagnoses, as these would constitute a book in their own right and are better covered with the assistance of qualified personnel. I will, however, cover the special considerations in respect of treatment, and while the principal concern must be to save life and aid recovery, it is necessary also to consider evacuation and the implications for the rest of the party of staying put.

Evacuation

Because the environment is frequently hostile, evacuation and the well-being of not only the casualty (or casualties) but also the other members of the party become major factors in considering treatment. Often the best treatment for the casualty compromises the overall safety of the party, and one must always keep this in mind when deciding what course of action to take. To stay put or to move on is the big question; however, in most cases it is usually better to try to move on and reach habitation. If you stay put, you have to find or construct a shelter (see page 100) and be able to keep everybody warm in temperatures that could easily reach 20°C below freezing. Somehow, too, the rescue services need to be alerted, and then they have to find you. If it is windy or the visibility is bad, helicopters may not be able to fly and it will take further time for help to reach you. Against this, however, you have to weigh up the problems of descending with an injured member of the party. This is made very much easier if you have a stretcher. There are a number available on the market that are not excessively heavy. They all work by using the

Above: This stretcher is easily carried in a pack and lends a day's adventure skiing an added degree of security. The rope is formed into three loops, allowing the bearers to control their load. The casualty is protected by a plastic survival bag.

Below: Emergency equipment for a day's wilderness skiing. Weighing 12lbs (5.5kg), it can be spread among the party. Stretcher, shovel, rope, first aid kit, sling, karabiner, survival bag, navigation equipment, and spare hat, gloves, top and glasses.

injured person's skis in some way. The casualty should be strapped in tightly with due allowance for both his or her injuries and mental well-being. It normally takes at least three people to handle a stretcher using a short length of rope. It is hard work but it is possible to descend quite difficult terrain and, bearing in mind the time it might take to get help, you can be saved a night in the open. Spending the night outside (see the section on snow-holing) is not necessarily the end of the world but it should certainly be avoided if at all possible. With this in mind it is an appropriate moment to consider the escalation factor.

The escalation factor

Accidents in our normal environments are bad enough, but when they occur in the wilderness there is so much more to consider. Simple incidents can lead quickly to serious complications for the inexperienced, and text-book procedures never seem to be adequate. For many, of course, this is an integral part of their enjoyment, knowing that whatever happens they will have to be self-reliant. The intensity of the experience heightens their enjoyment. All I can do is to make sure you understand what basic skills are required and to make you aware of the dangers. This is where the escalation factor comes in.

When you have to deal with an incident, even if at first it appears trivial, you must consider the consequences of all your actions. Let me take you through an imaginary scenario to illustrate what I mean.

The Val d'Isere—Tigne ski area in France is vast, one of the largest in the world, and offers many excellent wilderness routes that are well served by lifts. There is no restriction on skiing them and they are not patrolled. One of the best of these is the Col Pers route. A traverse and a short walk take you to the col, and before you is a tremendous bowl which eventually leads down to the Gorges de Malpasset. You follow this down until you reach the Pont St Charles, then you ski down the road to the village of Le Fornet. Once you cross the col you are committed, but it is nevertheless a popular route. Imagine you are skiing the route with a couple of friends, both good skiers. It is not the ideal number, more would be better, but it is also not an unreasonable number with which to find yourself. You reach the col at 1.30pm, a little late but you have been staying in Tigne at the other end of the systems and it has taken this long to get across. As you look down at the powder bowl it is too inviting to forego, and besides you have at least two and a half hours to spare and should even have time to catch the last lift back instead of taking the bus. You set off.

The first bowl is fantastic, beautiful powder. You then traverse for a short distance and are faced by another powder slope. The three of you whoop it up, but as you stop at the bottom you notice you are one short. Looking back up the slope you see your companion shaking powder from his hair. He is okay and waves to you. The sun is about to go behind the ridge so you decide to enjoy its last rays as he finds his ski. 'What a great day,' you think as you close your eyes and soak up the rays.

As soon as the sun drops from view, however, the temperature falls and you become impatient. 'Get a move on,' you shout. 'It's freezing down here.'

At last he finds his ski and quickly joins you. He looks tired; it has taken a lot of effort to dig for the ski but you are frozen stiff and time is getting on. You start down the next slope. This time two of you fall, your friend from his tiredness and you because you are cold. It doesn't take long to find your skis, however, and then the three of you start off again.

You soon reach the top of the gorge. Not far now, but the light is fading fast. In good light the gorge's twists and turns are great fun, but as the visibility deteriorates you stiffen with apprehension. Will we be able to see the rocks? Can we pick out the holes down to the river bed? Should we stop and find shelter so we don't hurt ourselves? The questions start to flood in. Your skiing slows to a snail's pace and you are now very cold . . .

Is it such an unreasonable scenario? Unfortunately not, and at this stage there have been no actual injuries, just a couple of minor incidents that have forced you into quite a difficult situation. There have been a lot of mistakes, of course, but what if, even had you started earlier, you had been unable to find

Below: What starts as fun can all too easily deteriorate.

your friend's ski or he had twisted his knee as he fell?

I am sure you would all have made it, but what is important is that you realise just how easily a situation can escalate and that no book or instructor can tell you how to cope with every scenario. Believe me, I am not trying to put you off. I simply wish to encourage you to be more responsible by showing you what decisions you might have to take and what areas of knowledge enable you to act wisely. Let us now tackle some of the situations for which I can offer concrete advice.

The body scan

Your first aid training should teach you to do a total body scan. This is a systematic check of the whole body that only takes a moment or two and helps you to ascertain the extent of any injuries. It is important because often the most serious injuries are not easily seen by the unpractised eye, especially if the casualty is unconscious or semi-conscious (a possibility in an avalanche accident). If you do not know how to carry out a body scan, get a medic to show you. The best medics for this are those with search and rescue training.

The avalanche victim

Most victims of an avalanche suffer from a number of traumatic conditions resulting from the impact of heavy lumps of snow; it is therefore necessary that each victim is examined thoroughly. Many are found unconscious, and unfortunately statistics suggest you should suspect a broken neck and handle with appropriate care.

If a victim is not breathing, you must clear the airways of snow as quickly as possible and perform mouth-to-mouth resuscitation (EAR).

Do not wait until you have completely uncovered the victim before starting treatment. As soon as the head and chest are clear, get to work on the breathing. If there is more than one person buried, you will have to decide whether to persist with resuscitation or search for the other(s); at this point the value of skiing in a large party becomes obvious. Resuscitation should, if

Above: Chamonix Guides practising a full body scan.

humanly possible, be continued until qualified personnel can take over. Once you have established that a victim is breathing unaided but is still unconscious, a plastic airway should be inserted to allow continued breathing. It may be possible to insert the airway to start with, which will prevent the need to bend the neck as severely as you would normally. Plastic airways are quite cheap but I suggest you get some training in their use; they need to be inserted upside down and then twisted into position. With the unconscious person breathing it only remains to maintain the passage of air and to keep the person as warm as possible.

At this point it may be wise to leave the victim partly buried while you attend to others. The snow will act as an insulator and the person will probably be warmer than if you remove him or her totally. With all avalanche victims, however, you must suspect a degree of hypothermia to have set in and act appropriately. This involves a gradual total rewarming rather than any localised rewarming. (See also the

section on cold-related injuries.) Shelter the person as best you can, insulated from the ground and, if possible, positioned between two fit people for the benefit to be had from their warmth. Providing there are no other serious injuries, the casualty can be fed and given hot drinks if you have any with you (but no alcohol!). Hypothermic victims are very difficult to resuscitate, and symptoms of other injuries may not be clear; nevertheless you must search for them.

Someone who suffers only mild hypothermia, once returned to normal, can be moved, although you must watch carefully as you continue your descent to make certain there is no relapse. If there are signs that the person's condition is worsening, repeat the warming process until he or she recovers again. Do so as often as is necessary to reach the bottom without the victim relapsing totally. It might save you an unpleasant night out.

Sprains, breaks and dislocations

All of these disorders require immobilisation so that the casualty can be moved. I recommend that your first aid kit contains a roll of sticky-backed, elasticised bandage at least 2in (5cm) wide. With this, some safety pins and a degree of ingenuity, most injuries can be immobilised.

Sprains and soft-tissue injuries

Try to ascertain how the accident happened as this may tell you in what direction a muscle or joint has been stressed. This is important because what you must do is strap the injury so as to strengthen the weakness. The sticky elastic bandage really comes into its own on such occasions. The strapping must be firm, but if you have to wrap the bandage right round a limb (and only do this as a last resort), be careful not to restrict the blood supply, especially in cold conditions when frostbite is a danger.

Breaks

Fractures are tackled in much the same way, with the main aim being immobilisation. Fortunately standard skiing equipment provides you with the means to improvise splints.

It should be possible to immobilise fractures of the upper body to such a degree that travel can be contemplated; indeed, it is important to do so (except in the case of neck and spine injuries). This can be unpleasant and extremely uncomfortable for the casualty, but is usually preferable to spending a very cold night out, when the escalation factor is sure to play its nasty part and endanger the whole party.

If you have a stretcher, you should also consider moving a casualty suffering from lower-limb fractures. Leave boots in place because they will offer warmth, though they may need loosening. Casualties with thigh fractures and pelvic injuries must not be moved because of the possibility of inflicting internal damage.

Right: Learning to reduce a shoulder dislocation. First Aid this serious need be considered only by the real wilderness skier.

Dislocations

Once a dislocation has been reduced, the limb concerned should always be immobilised. The longer a joint is dislocated the harder it becomes to reduce it. Some joints can be reduced easily while with others there is a strong possibility that the untrained will damage blood vessels and nerves in the process. You must consider the full implications of any action or lack of action. Once a dislocation is reduced and adequate immobilisation effected, it might be possible to continue your descent, and you must judge whether or not this is a sounder option than staying put, even though there is a risk of damaging the limb further.

Fingers

Finger dislocations can be reduced with a firm, straightening pull, and there are rarely any complications unless you pull so hard as to tear the overlying tendons. These will often be damaged anyway, and whether as a result of your pull or the injury it is difficult to know. Dislocation of a thumb is usually associated with a fracture at its base and consequently should just be immobilised.

Elbow

Dislocation of the elbow can be complicated as nerves and blood vessels run close to the joint and it is quite difficult to tell whether there is also a fracture. Before doing anything check to see if there is a pulse at the wrist and sensation in the hand. If there is, it is probably best to leave well alone, although swelling might cut off the pulse later. If pulse and sensation are not apparent, your actions are unlikely to worsen the situation and reduction can be considered. First of all examine the elbow and try to ascertain whether or not there is an associated fracture. If not, go ahead with a reduction – it will either happen easily or not at all. Lay the injured arm across the casualty's belly and pull firmly. As soon as it has been reduced, check for a pulse and sensation again. If these are not present, the joint should be separated again with traction and rotated slightly in order that the vessels and nerves are freed. The arm should then be splinted with the elbow bent at an angle of 90° and another check made for pulse and sensation. Medical assistance should be sought at the earliest opportunity.

Shoulder

Shoulder dislocation is one of the injuries most likely to result from a bad fall. There are a number of ways in which to reduce the dislocation but they all carry a risk of further damage to blood vessels and nerves. Unfortunately the quickest methods carry the highest risk. Methods involving continuous traction via a weight attached to the arm concerned are best but it usually takes upwards of an hour before the joint is reduced. The alternative is to apply a force with the help of an assistant. Care must be taken to pad any point of con-

tact between the first-aider and the patient so as to reduce the likelihood of further damage. There are two methods that can be tried:

1. With the patient lying down on his or her back, pull the arm downwards alongside the body. If counter rotation is required, it should be applied below the injured joint via a well-padded sling placed around the chest. The direction of pull for the counter rotation should be towards a point above the uninjured shoulder.

2. By placing a well-padded foot against the chest and pulling outwards and downwards, it may be possible to reduce the joint, but this carries with it a high risk of further damage.

Knee

Generally, major dislocations of the knee pop back into place of their own accord. The same procedure as for a dislocated elbow should then be followed, as damage to surrounding vessels and nerves is common. It is unlikely that the leg will be able to bear any weight, and it should be splinted to prevent further injury.

With all dislocations, remember that they are much more easily reduced if this can be done when the patient is still in shock. The longer you wait, the harder it will become.

Cold-related injuries

We have already considered hypothermia so I will now look at localised cold-related injuries, which are known as frostnip and frostbite. Frostnip is simply the first stage of frostbite and is not uncommon. It usually occurs when it is very cold and there is a strong wind. It appears as a blanching of the skin and is most commonly seen on the tip of the nose, around the nostrils, on the cheeks and ear lobes, and occasionally on the forehead and chin. It can also afflict fingertips and toes, although with modern boots this is becoming less of a problem. The solution is simply to warm the affected part as soon as the problem is diagnosed and then to keep it warm. With the face you can cup your hands around your mouth and blow warm air over the

frostnipped area. When the colour has returned, cover with a balaclava or scarf and keep checking to ensure it does not get worse. Hands can be warmed next to the body, as can feet. With feet, however, you are less likely to diagnose a problem as cold feet are not uncommon, and you will probably do more harm if you keep stopping and taking your boots off to check. If your feet do get very cold, loosen your boots and see if they get warmer.

Frostbite is more serious but there is little you can or should do on the mountainside. Again you have to consider the whole situation. Let's say that you do discover you have a frostbitten toe. If you stop to warm it and succeed in so doing, you must remain where you are and not use the foot. If, however, you do not warm the foot, you can continue to use it without causing much further injury. In other words, you can continue to use a frostbitten limb to ski down whereas once it has been warmed you are immobilised. Remember that prevention is better than cure, just as it is in the case of hypothermia.

Above: Frostnip on the cheek bone, a common site of affliction.

Cuts, abrasions and bleeding

You should treat these in just the same way as you would under any other circumstances. Any dressings you apply should be substantial enough to allow movement on the part of the patient.

Snowblindness

I shall finish this section with probably the most easily prevented injury – snowblindness. It is so easy to prevent and yet still afflicts even experienced skiers. The problem for the wilderness skier is that snowblindness leaves the casualty totally blind and reliant on the rest of the party to get him or her down. The implications of this need to be considered by all who value a suntan over their eyesight. Furthermore, it may take twelve hours or more for the symptoms to develop, so even if you take care during a tour, previous exposure may catch you out.

Glasses or goggles must always be worn as harmful UV light is present even on cloudy days and sometimes even when it is snowing. Spare glasses should be carried in case of loss or damage. Emergency goggles can be made out of card or similar material with a small pinhole for each eye. As a last resort use each eye alternately. Again, prevention is better than cure; buy good glasses or goggles and use them.

It will be clear by now that first aid in the mountain environment can be totally different from that to which you are probably used. It can involve many difficult decisions and a great deal of responsibility. I have outlined many measures that are normally left to trained personnel, but when you are alone in the wilderness their help may not be available, at least for some time. During that time the situation may worsen, endangering others. Having said that I hope I have not presented too gloomy a picture, because thousands of skiers do enjoy adventure skiing without incident. However, the potential is there, and I hope that you will now be better prepared to cope if you become one of the unfortunate few.

It has not been my intention to put you off, but I have been describing the realities that the wilderness skier should consider. If you have been deterred, I would certainly respect you far more for that than I would the skier who ventures forth in the expectation that someone else will risk all to rescue him or her in the event of trouble.

ROUTE FINDING

I am sure that there are many who have been skiing the powder for years with nothing more than a resort map and a blind faith that those before them knew where they were going. So why should you be any different and learn navigational skills?

The answer is twofold. In the first place consider the simple scenario of the weather changing, suddenly leaving you unable to pick out any longer the tracks that you were following. In the second, why follow others anyway? With some navigational knowledge not only can you seek out new terrain to ski but also you can assess which is the safest line to take and determine where the best snow may lie. If you have got this far in the book and are still enthusiastic, the chances are that you have an adventurous nature, and I am sure that the feeling of being even more independent will appeal.

I will use the same approach to this section as I did to the last and point out those skills that are important to the wilderness skier. I will have to rely on you to learn the basics from other sources, as to include these would require almost another book.

Below: When conditions get this bad, do not lose sight of your companions and be sure that you can navigate.

Maps
Navigation starts with the map. Resort maps vary from very accurate to hopeless, but even at their best they can be used only for visual reference. However, most ski areas are also covered by properly surveyed maps. The best scale is 1:25,000, although 1:50,000 can also be used. These maps show contours, which you should be able to interpret accurately while making allowances for the snow cover. This is not difficult but does require practice, and is the basis of good navigation. You can relate the map to terrain and assess where you are. The contours also tell you the shapes of the slopes themselves, and this can be very useful in determining how safe a slope may be. Remember that concave slopes are safer than convex ones. The density of the contours indicates the steepness of a slope. It is possible to work this out quite accurately, but it takes time and does not allow for localised variations; nevertheless, an indication can be useful.

Maps show which way is north, and from this you are able to determine the aspect of all slopes (the direction in which they face). With knowledge of avalanches and the recent weather, this helps you determine which slopes present most risk as well as which might hold the best powder. Maps also indicate the location of cliffs and major crevasses.

Compass
Maps on there own, however, are not enough, especially when visibility goes. Then you are faced with two problems; first, how to proceed accurately in any one direction; and second, how to assess the distance you have come. To move in a particular direction when visibility is poor, you need to use a compass to take a bearing from your map and then to ski along that bearing. Care must be taken, however, because no matter how good a compass is there will always be error. At best you can only hope to be within a couple of degrees of the direction you wish to follow. If you realise this, you can make allowances when you plan your route.

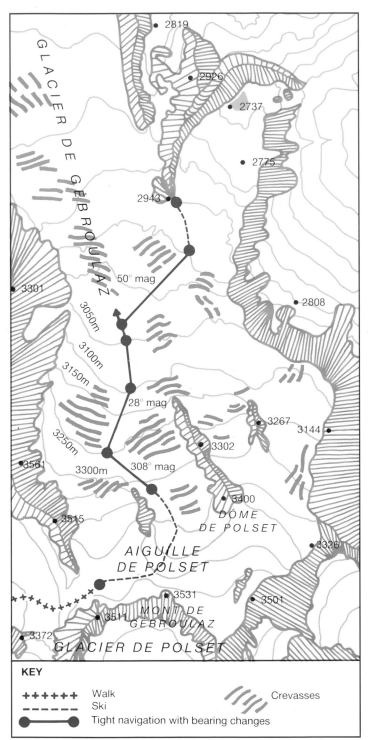

Map labels:

GLACIER DE GÉBROULAZ

2819
2926
2737
2775
2943
50° mag
3301
3050m
2808
3100m
3150m
28° mag
3267
3144
3302
3250m
3561
308° mag
3300m
3400
DÔME DE POLSET
3515
3326
AIGUILLE DE POLSET
3531
3501
3511
MONT DE GÉBROULAZ
3372
GLACIER DE POLSET

KEY

++++++ Walk
- - - - - - Ski
●━━━━● Tight navigation with bearing changes

///// Crevasses

Altimeter

Assessing distance is very difficult on skis because we all ski at different and inconsistent speeds, and we usually assess distance as a factor of our speed over the terrain. To overcome this problem the skier can use an altimeter. Let me describe an actual route to show you how to solve a typical navigational problem.

The region known as the Trois Vallées in France is one of the largest ski areas in the world, and has a number of excellent wilderness ski routes that can be approached via the lift system and are skiable in a single day. One of the wildest is the Glacier de Gébroulaz. It is approached from the top of the Telesiege du Col in the Val Thorens system. From the top station an hour's walk and climb takes you to the Col de Gébroulaz, and from here a great run takes you back eventually to Meribel. However, the top part of the glacier is cut by a number of crevasses, and careful navigation is required if these are to be avoided. You have checked locally and been told that all but the very largest are full of snow. When the light is good, this will cause you no problems as you can see most of the difficulties, and indeed it

Above: Map, compass, altimeter.

Left: Even the most difficult of navigational problems can be solved with the right tools. This route down the Glacier de Gébroulaz is described in detail in the text.

Right: Skiing on an accurate bearing in a whiteout requires at least two, and preferably three, people. Both, or all three, move along the same bearing, the rear skier(s) correcting the one(s) in front.

would be foolish to set off in bad weather. The weather in the mountains, however, is not always predictable, and cloud can often descend quickly, making visibility poor.

At the top of the col you check that your altimeter is reading correctly at 3434m. (Altimeters work on air pressure and should be checked at every opportunity and recalibrated if necessary.) The weather looks good, and from the map you can see that, although the first bowl appears fine, there are crevasses running all the way across it at about 3300m. You could head across to the third bowl below the Dôme de Polset but decide that the second looks better. At the top of this bowl you check the snow-pack for any avalanche potential. It's okay, so you can proceed; but no sooner have you started than a cloud comes in over the ridge to the west. You think it will probably clear, but for the moment the visibility is very poor and you know that you will have to pass by the crevasses soon. From the map you can see that there are a few at an altitude of 3330m. If you stay on the small ridge and keep the rocks to your left close by, you will miss these.

SKIING ON A COMPASS BEARING

To avoid the next batch, however, will need tighter navigation.

From a height of 3300m you leave the 'handrail' of the rocks and have to head across for the gap through the next band of crevasses. The slope here faces at 308° (magnetic). You ski down on this bearing to an altitude of 3250m, using the other members of the group to ensure you stay on bearing. By this time your altimeter may not be reading so accurately because of the changing weather; you have no means of knowing but all you have to do is to allow greater leeway. Having reached a height of 3250m, the slope starts facing towards the north and you are able to ski on a magnetic bearing of 28° to a height of 3100m. You now have a clear descent to a height of 3050m if you stay in the faint valley. Here you have to consider how you are going to avoid the next cluster of crevasses. You descend another 20m, then take a bearing on the direction of the fall-line. By putting this bearing on the map (allowing for magnetic variation) and finding where it crosses the contours at an angle of 90°, you are able to assess approximately where you are. From this point you take a bearing that allows you to ski to the north-east through the obvious gap. As you proceed you take notice of the way in which the slope changes, then you cross a very flat area where you end up walking for a short while. As soon as the slope steepens you check your altimeter again and continue down to 2950m. Now you traverse towards point 2943, making sure you do not drop below 2930m. From here the descent is free of crevasses.

What I have described here is one of the trickiest problems you are likely to encounter. You would only embark on such a route confident that all but the very biggest crevasses were filled with snow anyway, but even then you would not flirt with unnecessary danger and would still choose the safest line.

Your navigational ability is as much a factor to be considered in choosing which runs to ski as your skiing prowess. The greater your ability, the more ambitious and adventurous you can be.

SNOW-HOLING

We have looked at a number of fairly dire situations in which we all hope we will never find ourselves. We could be unfortunate, however, and I hope that the information I have presented will make you feel more confident about what to do in an emergency. Up until now I have argued in favour of descending when trouble strikes because during a night out in winter any incident can escalate into something altogether more serious. But what do you do if you have to spend the night out?

The answer is to snow-hole. The committed wilderness skier may even choose to snow-hole on a long tour. With a good sleeping bag, a stove, food and drink it can be a great experience. That, however, is really a different game, and what you may have to do is to survive without these extras. A snow-hole is still the answer. Inside the temperature hovers around freezing but you are insulated from any wind, and although you will be chilly you should certainly survive. Survival is 90 per cent a state of mind, anyway; it takes determination and a strong will. Having said that, let us make the other 10 per cent as favourable as possible.

Below: Sometimes the entrance to a snow-hole needs to be built up with blocks of snow.

The type of snow-hole you build depends upon the state of the snow. They all take quite some time to build so the decision whether or not to snow-hole must be taken early. If the snow is soft and does not support a hole, pile heaps upon heaps and allow it to settle. Once it has settled you can dig into it. Hard snow may be cut into blocks with the edge of a ski. The blocks can then be built up around your excavation site to create a hole. Most probably, however, you will be able to dig into the snow with your shovel. Find a good, deep bank of snow and dig in horizontally, keeping the hole as small as possible. It is a good thing to remove some of your inner layers of clothing before you dig as it is generally hot work. If you sweat a lot, you will regret it as you cool down later on unless you have some dry clothes to put on after you have finished digging. If there are two of you with shovels, a parallel tunnel can be dug to the side. How far you go in depends on the steepness of the snow bank and how many are to fit inside, but when you have reached the required depth turn sideways and start to dig out the main chamber. This should be just big enough to house the party and should have a trench near the entrance so that the cold air has somewhere to sink, leaving the warmer air above where you will be sat. Scrape the walls as smooth as possible as small drops of water will drip annoyingly from any protuberances. The actual design of the interior can be left to your architectural talents and helps to pass the night hours away.

The entrance can be blocked but an airway must be kept clear, particularly if it is snowing outside. The most frequent cause of accidents in snow-holes is inadequate ventilation. Care must always be taken to ensure a passage of air, and any headaches among the party may indicate that it is insufficient. A shovel should be kept inside just in case the snow-hole collapses. Outside it is a good thing to mark the snow-hole clearly so that if anyone has to go out, they can easily find it again. Shouting to the occupants is useless as snow is an excellent sound insulator. When

SNOW-HOLING

Ingenuity is called for in designing a shelter in the snow.

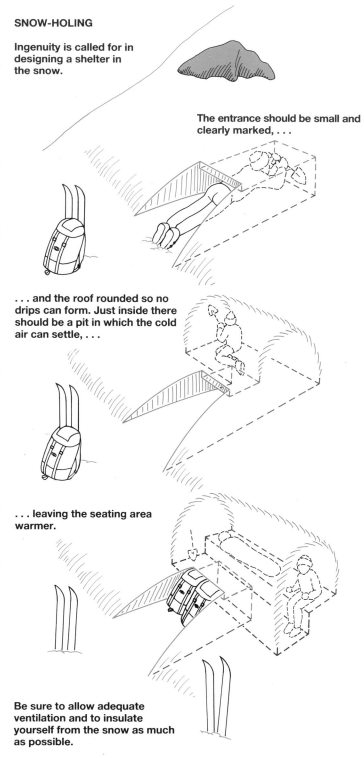

The entrance should be small and clearly marked, . . .

. . . and the roof rounded so no drips can form. Just inside there should be a pit in which the cold air can settle, . . .

. . . leaving the seating area warmer.

Be sure to allow adequate ventilation and to insulate yourself from the snow as much as possible.

you enter the hole, always brush off any snow from your clothing as it will melt in the warmer air inside, making you damp. As you settle for the night, use each other's body warmth and insulate yourselves from the floor with whatever is available. Loosen your boots to improve the circulation in your feet and take it in turns to be on the outside of the huddle. Be sensitive to your extremities and if they are getting chilled, use your own or someone else's body warmth to keep them warm. Survival needs to be worked at.

I hope you are never forced to snow-hole, but if you are, make every effort to follow sound practice. Effort early on could even turn it into an almost pleasurable experience!

ENVIRONMENTAL CONSIDERATIONS

The ecology of the alpine wilderness is delicately balanced. A large number of plants and animals survive in this beautiful, harsh environment, but only just! Your presence can barely be tolerated and it is therefore important that you ski sensitively.

Below: The alpine environment is full of life even in winter. This is a white-tailed jackrabbit in a snow hide.

Bottom: Have you ever wondered what made the tracks you come across in the snow?

Make sure that you take out what you take in. Rubbish buried in the snow will, by the summer, be rubbish on the ground. We must all take individual responsibility.

The animals that live in the snow are very sensitive, timid creatures and are easily scared by passing skiers, especially if they are whooping it up. This is particularly important to bear in mind if you are skiing below the tree line. It is difficult to check yourself when the powder is deep and it is the best day you have had for a long time; you want to let the whole world know just how good it is. But ask yourself if the world really cares. It is your day, so enjoy it yourself; that should be enough.

The tree line is also a critical area for plant life, especially young, budding trees which are easily snapped and broken by passing skiers. Not only does this prevent the full growth of the trees but it also destroys a part of the animals' habitat. Remember it is a very delicately balanced ecology. Every part is intimately dependent on every other, and our presence can so easily upset the balance.

The experience of wilderness skiing can be greatly enhanced if you get in touch with the environment. Take some time out from the downhill rush and enjoy the silence of the snow. Contemplate what sort of animal made the tracks you can see and what it might think of you. Some years ago I was teaching a group of 'massive miles' skiers, skiers who just wanted to clock up as many feet of descent as possible. We were clambering along a high ridge trying to reach some fresh-looking powder when we were confronted by a small stoat peeking over a rock. Suddenly, to my surprise and pleasure, the miles were no longer important as we watched this tiny animal in its winter coat scamper from rock to rock. It seemed to be as fascinated by us as we were by it. Finally we moved on in silence, and the group's skiing attained a degree of sensitivity that I knew I could never have brought about on my own. Advanced skiing is not solely about technical excellence.

CHAPTER 6

COMPETITION FUN

This book has been written for the recreational skier, not the budding instructor or racer, but should recreational skiers deny themselves the pleasure and fun of competition? The answer is obviously no, and I am sure many of you have already raced at one level or another.

There is no doubt that competing in any of the disciplines can be a very positive experience, especially at your level of expertise, but equally, with the wrong approach, it can be devastating. In order to make the most of competition I believe you should start by asking yourself why you have chosen to race.

One of the many pleasures of any athletic performance comes from the feeling that you are improving. This may be improvement compared to your last run or yesterday's run, or in the longer continuum of your skiing life. It is not the sole motivation, but one of the joys of our sport is the diversity of avenues it offers from which we can derive pleasure. Measuring improvement can take many forms, such as skiing steeper slopes or hairier bump fields, but one of the most straightforward is to run the poles of a race course. 'Why race against others, then?' some of you may ask. 'Surely it is only the time which is important.' In a sense this is true, but because there are so many variables involved, such as the course, the snow and

the weather, we can never be sure that we have actually improved. By using others to measure ourselves against we are able to rationalise many of the variables. Competing only to win can be a very negative experience, whereas competing only to improve can be of great value. If you do not improve, you can analyse why, make adjustments to your skiing and turn a failure into a positive experience.

Competition fun can be had from nearly every aspect of the sport but the classic way to compete is to run the poles. The discipline of turning according to the dictates of a well-designed course will benefit nearly every skier. In the following pages all I am going to attempt is to inspire you to have a go. By this stage of the book your technical base should be good and you should be more than able to put in a creditable performance. Whole books have been dedicated to the intricacies of racing techniques, and much of what has been described in this book springs from observations made by racing coaches. If the racing bug bites you, I suggest you read more widely and join a club where you will receive specific coaching.

Below: A duel slalom NASTAR race at Keystone in Colorado, suitable for all standards.

GIANT SLALOM

The giant slalom is the best discipline with which to start your racing as the turns closely resemble those with which you commonly have to contend in free skiing. The course can be up to three quarters of a mile in length and the gates consist of two 'posts', each made from a rectangle of cloth supported by two poles. The gates are alternately red and blue in colour and are in one of three configurations. Horizontal gates and vertical gates are as their names suggest relative to the fall-line. Oblique gates are off-set across the fall-line. Good courses are not necessarily difficult to ski but en-courage fast, smooth skiing which makes full use of the natural variations of the terrain.

The line

As I am sure many of you are already aware, it is not simply a case of skiing up to a gate and turning. If you do this, you will blow out after only a few turns and be unable to stay on the course. Solving this problem is fairly straightforward. The secret is to turn *above* each gate so that at least two thirds of the turn is completed as you pass through it. Any slowing down should be done

Below: A women's giant slalom.

before the commencement of a fresh turn, not during it.

To help you ski the best line, I would like to remind you how you skied through the trees, looking for the gaps rather than the trees. It is just the same during a giant slalom run. As you look ahead, see the gaps through which you have to ski rather than the poles around which you have to turn. Adopting this approach may be sufficient on its own to get you skiing the correct line. The line should take you close to the poles, so much so that you even brush them, but you should never hit them in a manner that disturbs your balance.

The next tactic for ensuring you

take the right line is to inspect the course before skiing it. It is claimed that the very best skiers are able to remember the whole course in detail, but for most of us three or four gates at a time is realistically all we can expect of ourselves. As you inspect the course try to get a feel for its speed. Noting where it slows down and where it is quick is of more value than remembering individual gate sequences unless there is something very particular to remember. Judging the speed of each section allows you to make adjustments to your line in accordance with any variation. As your technique and athletic prowess improve, so you will be able to ski a tighter line through each gate with no loss of speed, and this will improve your time over the whole course.

Techniques

GS turns are fast and flowing. They make full use of the skills acquired in mastering speed control. There are times when you want to slow down by rounding out your turns, and times when you want to speed up either by skiing a tighter line or by adding power to your turns. Any dynamic stepping on the approach to a turn should take place early to prevent the forward projection of the body pushing the supporting ski backwards, thereby defeating the object. Parallel step turns and scissor step turns are frequently used to adjust the line of approach. Applying all these techniques correctly and skilfully can be achieved only through practice.

The giant slalom gives you the opportunity to ski at speed and to enjoy turning at speed. The dictates of the course ensure that you ski with precision, and by pitting yourself against others you get immediate feedback as to how well you are fine-tuning your skiing skills.

Below: Notice the similarities between the technique employed in this women's giant slalom and those in 'Cruising with Style'.

SLALOM

Slalom skiing feels quite different from GS because the course is much tighter and sharper; however, the same principles apply to the course design in that it should not be difficult to ski. It should promote flowing, rhythmical skiing with a number of rhythm changes during the course of a run. The gates each consist of two poles with flags on them and are arranged in configurations similar to those in the GS. Horizontally placed gates are known as open gates and vertically placed gates as closed. Oblique gates are called

will experience initially will spring from an inappropriate choice of line. There is no single perfect line on a course; the line that is best for you is dependent on your individual style of skiing. It should take you close to the poles again, and with their modern flexible bases you will need to deflect them. This should be done in a manner that does not interfere with your balance, however.

Below: The drama of the start gate.

Below right: Slalom racing.

has been slower than expected. Their second run, if they manage to stay on the course, is usually faster because they are skiing closer to their limit.

Technique
Some of the techniques we have discussed are totally inappropriate for racing, and the slalom in particular, because the philosophy behind them is the enjoyment of movement, and often they have been developed at the expense of efficiency and economy of movement. They will, however, improve your technical base. Your balance

the same. Many other terms are applied which refer to collective patterns of gates, such as off-set hairpins and verticalies; however, these vary from country to country. Much of what I have said in the section on the giant slalom also applies here.

The line
The line is ever important and the principle of aiming for the gaps still applies. Many of the problems you

One of the major problems facing slalom competitors is the control of speed. It is usually easy to keep accelerating on a course but you quickly reach a speed above which you cannot cope. This applies equally to the very best of skiers, but what they are able to do is to judge the maximum speed at which they can ski without blowing out and ski just below that. You can observe this when you watch slalom skiers in a race after their first run responses will be taken to their limits and you will understand your skiing better. This will make the transition to the efficient, economic techniques of the slalom racer easier.

Many of the techniques are, of course, still applicable, particularly those you have applied to the bumps. Here the 'rules' were very similar, and it is noticeable that good bump skiers are also usually good slalom skiers and vice-versa.

The main difference between slalom and giant slalom is the quickness of action and reaction demanded by the former. You can train for this in your normal free skiing by quickening the tempo of your turns, but do remember to vary the rhythm. Changing from edge to edge as sharply as possible will program your muscular responses to the demands of the slalom course. You should practise this in as variable conditions as possible, because turning quickness (as opposed to speed down the course) is dependent on co-ordination. Co-ordination is improved by skiing in a relaxed manner because only the active muscles are tense; the inactive muscles are relaxed, allowing rapid movement by the others. It is also worth bearing in mind that quickness is not achieved through aggressive action. Aggressiveness results in too harsh an action; subtle, sharp actions are more effective.

Finally, let me say that one of the biggest influences on your times in both GS and slalom will be your desire, or otherwise, to go faster. Just wanting to go faster will almost certainly improve your times, and this means that you need to enjoy speed. Enjoying speed is definitely a prerequisite for participation in the next two disciplines.

DOWNHILL AND THE FLYING K

I have already described how skiing at speed can sharpen your awareness and focus your concentration, and what better opportunity to ski fast than to run a downhill course. Unfortunately it is very difficult for the recreational skier to get the chance to do just that; it is possible, however, to run a flying k at a number of resorts. This is a straight course on which you can schuss at maximum speed and have your speed measured accurately; it also allows you to experiment with your tuck position. More than that, however, it accustoms you to travelling at high speeds and allows you to discover terminal velocity. Because air resistance increases as the square of speed, for any constant slope and body position there is a speed at which you will plateau. Becoming comfortable with that speed is a significant step forward.

It is not merely a matter of technique, as I am sure you can imagine. When you are travelling at high speed, it is important that your mind does not disturb the natural balance of your body. Build up your speed threshold steadily, making use of those days when you feel good. Take every opportunity on the slopes to ski quickly, always bearing in mind other users, of course.

Most people faced with a fast schuss automatically drop into an egg position for greater speed. This is fine until you need to slow down, when your first reaction should be to use your body as a wind check. (You can decrease your speed by as much as 10–25mph by doing this.) If you have not practised skiing at speed in a high stance, however, this will be difficult.

Both the flying k and the downhill can be dangerous and the consequences of a fall serious, but the joy of travelling at maximum speed is said by many to be the very essence of skiing. As you will have gathered, I am not one of those, and although I do on occasion value speed, I value equally the quality of movement. The next discipline is centred around the quality of, and the sensation derived from, body movement as opposed to speed. It is the discipline of freestyle.

Right: The flying kilometre.

Below: The downhill.

FREESTYLE SKIING

There are three disciplines in free-style competition: the moguls (skiing the bumps), ballet and aerials.

Mogul competitions are about skiing quickly through the bumps. The score is calculated according to speed, style and a couple of jumps *en route*. The course itself is usually constructed by the competitors, who ski it over a number of days forming their own bumps.

Ballet is very similar to ice dance. The run is choreographed to music of the competitor's choice, and marks are awarded for artistic merit as well as technical difficulty.

The aerials are performed on a specially constructed site. This includes not only carefully designed kickers to launch the competitors on their jumps but also a steep, soft landing area. You should only train for this event under the supervision of a fully qualified coach.

There is no doubt in my mind that

there is tremendous value to be had from freestyle skiing. The bumps speak for themselves, as do the aerials, but the value of ballet may need a little explaining. In the first place it is very enjoyable. Skiing to music and abandoning your body to new shapes and forms is pleasurable and, with many of the man- oeuvres, exciting. You have to use every part of the ski and learn to balance in positions which hitherto have been completely alien. Furthermore, the flexibility and suppleness that you develop can only do you good. Many of the manoeuvres may look very difficult but you will be surprised at how quickly you can put together a simple routine. It is certainly worth having a go but, again, it is best to do so under trained supervision.

Below and bottom: The mogul competition is one of the most exciting to watch.

Above: The aerials. Points are awarded for the take-off, height, style, precision and landing.

Left and below: Julia Snell, a world-class performer, exhibits both the grace and athleticism of ski ballet.

CHAPTER 7

ALTERNATIVE GAMES

As an advanced skier you will be of well-developed athletic ability and have the snow world before you as your proverbial oyster. Over the years a variety of skiing alternatives have been developed to allow us to enjoy this world even more fully. Some have been passing fads, others have stayed. Most of them are fun in their own right and all of them can help you to develop your dynamic balance along the way. To finish with, I would like to present some of these alternative games – not in great detail but just enough, I hope, to inspire you.

Below: Monoskiing in soft snow.

MONOSKIING

Monoskiing comes and goes. Sometimes it gets good press, other times bad. Whichever, it has its devotees and I am one of them. For me the monoski is very definitely an off-piste tool. I accept that many use it on the prepared slopes and even race with it, for but me it really comes into its own when used in snow as nature provided it.

The monoski can be skied in a variety of ways. To start with just use your normal skiing techniques and after a very short time you should be able to handle it enough to start appreciating its virtues. It is a pig to traverse with so concentrate

on linked rhythmical turns. But what is it that makes it so special for me? It isn't just that it is easy to use in the powder and other 'real' snows, but that it encourages you to look at and ski the terrain in an entirely new way.

Long, curving, elegant lines are the call of the day rather than the rhythmical short turns you would normally use. Make the most of the terrain in the sense of using banks and hollows to control your speed. New manoeuvres are possible, such as upside-downers, tail stalls and re-entries. A new stance can be developed which will give you sensations completely different from those you are used to. This different perception of what you can do can rub off on your normal two-footed skiing and open up new horizons there as well. Do not worry about the monoski harming your technique; at your level this is very unlikely. A short transitional phase will always be necessary but will not slow your progress much more than changing from slalom skis to giant slalom skis (and skiing them well), for example.

If you have the opportunity to try monoskiing and are prepared to give it a day or two, I am sure you will not be disappointed provided you heed a couple of suggestions.

Terrain
Choose your terrain carefully. You need a medium-steep slope, one which you would be prepared to schuss. Preferably it would be covered with soft snow. You need also to consider the uplift. Chairs and enclosed lifts are the easiest but drag lifts can be ridden with practice. Finally, make sure the run continues right back to the lift. Monos cannot be skated along the flat and unless you judge your terrain well you could end up walking. This needs careful consideration if you are skiing away from the prepared slopes, as walking any distance through powder is one of the most demoralising experiences there is in skiing.

Equipment

Choose a ski about as long as you are tall. You do not need extra length because of the width.

Technique

The best turns to start with are hip cross-overs. The most common mistake is not to ski fast enough. The mono feels unstable at slow speeds. If you find you need the poles excessively, this also is an indication that you are skiing too slowly. Getting up after a fall can be tiring because your feet are not independent, so use your poles crossed for extra support and fix the uphill foot first if it has come off.

These are just some hints to get you going. See 'Further Reading' as there have been books written solely for the monoskier. Alternatively, seek specialised instruction. Do not put monoskiing in the same ranks as the hoola-hoop. It is not a passing fad and has much to offer. Apart from any other consideration monoskiing is great fun, especially if you are learning it in a group of like-minded friends.

CLASSIC MONOSKIING STANCE

This is completely different from stances covered so far.

Below: The mono encourages you to take different lines.

Bottom: The mono stance is a lot of fun.

SNOWBOARDING

Snowboarding is undoubtedly the craze of the moment, but will it last? I think it will because it is so entirely different from skiing. It takes place in the same environment but there the similarity ends. The movements and the stance are completely different, being more akin to those of surfing or skateboarding. It has been around for longer than many people realise, but the original boards had no edges and could be used only in deep, soft snow. With the advent of edges the snowboard could be used anywhere and is now a constant sight in many resorts.

Equipment

There are many designs of board around but I suggest that the standard hire board will be adequate for your first few attempts; do be sure, though, that it has metal edges as there are still a few around from the days when they did not have them. The bindings vary in that some are designed for use with soft boots and others for use with ski boots or specialised snowboarding boots which resemble ski mountaineering boots. Unfortunately none of them (at the time of writing) release in a fall, though I understand many binding manufacturers are trying to solve this problem. The danger is that as you fall you may dig your knees into the snow and twist them. To deny that this is a possibility would be wrong of me, but whether there is more risk of injury than in skiing is difficult to tell.

Terrain

Many of the criteria we applied in the choice of terrain for the mono should be applied in the case of the snowboard; in addition, though, an easy prepared slope is also fine. All forms of uplift can be used but drag lifts are the most difficult. As with the mono, the snowboard is unstable at low speeds so the slope should not be too shallow.

Right: The craze of the moment. A combination of skiing and surfing, snowboarding is particularly fun in the powder.

Technique

Your highly developed dynamic balance will help you, but snowboarding is so different from skiing that unless you have surfed or skateboarded it may be like starting totally afresh. There are two ways to stand on a board: leading with your left foot, which is known as the natural stance, and leading with your right, which is known as the goofy stance. Neither has any advantage over the other, so go with what feels natural. Most bindings can be adjusted to either stance.

There are basically two types of turn, frontside and backside, but both are tackled in a very similar fashion. The important thing to start with is that you stand over the front foot. With the pressure distributed evenly over this foot, you can change direction by swinging the back of the board around with the other foot. The degree of banking will vary with speed and conditions. Initially your turns will be very skidded, but as you become more confident and competent so you will use the edge more and distribute your weight more evenly between your feet.

A snowboard is tremendous fun in the powder and, again, this is where I prefer to use it. The techniques are the same although you can start turning with a pure banking movement probably earlier in good powder than you can on harder snow.

As with the mono the line you take is quite different. You must search for undulations in the snow where you can use the shape of the land to control your speed. Banks are a favourite because you can ride them just like waves on the sea.

Like monoskiing, snowboarding can give you an entirely new perspective on what is possible, and that is justification enough to encourage you to give it a go.

Below: Snowboarding is here to stay and already has structured competitions.

TELEMARKING

Telemarking has been around since the birth of skiing and was probably one of the first techniques to be used to turn on downhill descents. It comes from a field of skiing known as Nordic skiing or free-heel skiing, the distinctive factor being that, unlike in alpine skiing, the heel of the boot is not fixed to the ski. In recent years telemarking (the term generally refers to the use of a beefed-up version of the cross-country ski) has gained popularity among alpine skiers looking for something different. The whole discipline of Nordic skiing has much to offer, but here I will restrict myself to talking about telemarking because that is the area I suspect most of you would like to try.

Equipment

Telemarking skis lie halfway between cross-country skis and alpine skis. They have edges, but are thinner and significantly lighter than alpine skis, especially when considered with the binding. The telemark binding is known as a three-pin, there being three pins which fit into holes on the front of the boot. There are a number of elaborations to this basic arrangement – some bindings have a release mechanism, others a cable for greater retention – but for your first foray into this activity the standard three-pin will be sufficient.

Above: Telemark equipment can be used on the groomed slopes, in the bumps and in the wilderness.

Below: Telemarking can open the way to many new sensations and is certainly worth trying.

The boots are generally made of leather with a rubber, vibram sole. The closer they fit and the more support they offer, the better. Specialised poles are available but normal alpine ones will suffice to start with.

There is a great deal more to the equipment than I have outlined here but this should be enough to get you going. I am also assuming that you will use the uplift of the resort at this stage, and for that reason I have not mentioned anything about skins and waxes. Once you are hooked you can find out how to use this equipment for uphill walking as well. The potential of telemarking for wilderness skiing is already being well exploited by many.

THE TELEMARK TURN

Start with your skis in a wedge and allow the inside ski to fall back so you are standing on the ball of that foot (1). As you steer around the turn, your skis can become parallel, although the inside foot should remain behind the outside foot (2). To change direction, step the inside ski forwards, transferring your

Terrain
For your first few runs choose an easy slope, preferably with good snow. Avoid the bumps and narrow trails until you are confident. Using the uplift is straightforward and should cause you no problems.

Technique
You will find that with little extra effort you can ski quite normally on telemark equipment, certainly on easy terrain. Many types of parallel turns can be performed and the benefits to your balance are enormous. It is, however, the telemark turn itself that is of most interest as it is so different from alpine skiing.

Done well it is a very elegant way of turning, and there are many vari-

ations. Start in a wedge position and as you go around a turn allow your inside leg to drop so that you are on the ball of your foot on that ski. The tip of the ski will end up about level with the middle of your other foot. To change direction stand up in a wedge and repeat the movement to the other side. As you become more proficient you will be able to omit the wedge position completely.

Telemarking can not only open up the wilderness but it involves a whole new body language which is fun in its own right. What I have described here is but a crumb from a large cake, but I hope that crumb will give you a taste for the rest of the cake.

balance so you feel you are standing on the inside of the ski. The degree of wedging will vary according to experience.

SKI MOUNTAINEERING

Ski mountaineering is the natural extension of the adventure skiing we have already examined in detail. Using skins attached to the bases of your skis and special bindings, it is possible to explore the mountains. This aspect of skiing seems to be going in two directions.

Traditionally ski mountaineers were mountaineers who used skis to help them climb mountains, but in recent years many skiers have been using the same equipment and techniques in order to reach better skiing fields. Both applications, of course, are equally valid.

I have already stressed the importance of being totally self-reliant in the wilderness. For the ski mountaineer it is absolutely vital. In spite of the necessity for this commitment, many are taking to this area of the sport in an effort to escape the crowded ski resorts.

Equipment

Ski mountaineering unfortunately needs quite a lot of specialised equipment. Your skis can remain the same but you need different bindings. Ski mountaineering bind-ings have a heel that can be either fixed (for downhill skiing) or free (for climbing up). You need skins, which are fixed as I described in Chapter 4. Rear-entry boots are being used more and more for touring because they are reasonably comfortable to walk in and, of course, great to ski in. The only time they are not suitable is when you have to do any climbing *en route.* You may also need crampons and an ice-axe. If you enter glaciated terrain, you also need a climbing harness and rope. In addition, you need all the equipment I have recommended already for adventure skiing. Many ski mountaineering routes require you to spend nights in mountain huts or even snow-holes, in which case you need sleeping bags, stoves and food. Finally, in order to carry all this equipment you must have a good sack. This may sound daunting but you will be surprised how quickly your sack becomes a part of you. Fortunately much of the equipment I have mentioned can usually be hired.

Below: For a real appreciation of mountains, try ski mountaineering.

Location

Ski mountaineering can be and is indulged in all over the world, from the Scottish highlands to the high mountains of the Himalayas. All you need is the right companions and the right skills.

Skills

To ski mountaineer safely and responsibly you need a number of additional skills; to acquire these you can join one of the many courses advertised. Alternatively you can always hire an internationally qualified mountain guide. The following is a check-list of the skills which are necessary to ski mountaineer in the high mountains.

1. Skiing ability. As an advanced skier used to skiing away from the prepared tracks, this should cause you no difficulty. However, it is the ability to pick yourself up after a fall and get on with the descent which is most important. The mountains have little respect for style; function and determination are far more important.

Below: You also need to be able to enjoy the climb.

2. Climbing ability. You should certainly know how to handle an ice-axe and be able to use crampons. These skills are not difficult to acquire, particularly to the level necessary for ski mountaineering. You should also be able to handle rope – to tie the right knots (there are not very many), to belay and to anchor yourself to the mountain. Again, the techniques involved are not as difficult to learn as you may think, although their skilful application does take experience.

3. Navigation. It is essential that you are able to navigate confidently in the mountains.

4. Crevasses. You will frequently have to pass through crevassed areas and must know how to extricate yourself or others from a crevasse using the equipment you have with you.

5. Survival. There is the real possibility that the undertaking of your own rescue could escalate into an even more serious incident, and you have to ask if it is fair or indeed ethically right to expect the rescue services to help you. To me the very essence of the sport is to be out there alone (with the rest of your party, of course) and to be totally self-reliant. With this philosophy you need to be sure that you know how to survive in what can be a very hostile environment.

6. Avalanches. The ability to assess the danger from avalanches is vital to all ski mountaineers. Similarly, you must know what to do in the event of being involved in an avalanche.

Many of these points apply equally to the adventure skier, so the transition to ski mountaineering may not be as great as you first think. However (and this may sound clichéd), because ski mountaineering generally does demand more of you, the rewards also seem more intense. It is a great aspect of the varied and wide-ranging sport of sliding around the snowy slopes which we call skiing. It is also, perhaps, one of the closest to the origins of the sport.

Right: Many skills are needed to ski mountaineer safely.

GLOSSARY

anchoring securing oneself to the mountainside.

angulation refers to the way in which the hips are dropped to the inside of a turn (hip angulation) and to the medial movement of the knees as a fine-tuning movement (knee angulation).

anticipation a preparatory rotation of the upper body in the direction of a new turn.

banking leaning towards the inside of a turn.

basket the ring, usually plastic, on the bottom of a ski pole to prevent it from sinking too far into the snow.

belaying the making fast of a rope at one end so that a person attached to the other cannot fall.

bumps a series of hummocks in the snow formed by the passage of numerous skiers; moguls.

canting lateral adjustment to boots, skis or bindings which allows the skier to stand evenly.

check a sudden edging action which provides a platform.

compression turns a versatile method of turning that involves flexing the legs.

cornice an overhanging crest of snow formed by wind on the lee side of a ridge.

crampons spikes worn on boots to give grip on ice.

crevasse a crack in a glacier caused by the ice flowing over a convex slope.

cross-country a form of skiing using lighter equipment than alpine skiing and also different techniques.

cross-over the action of moving the body across the line of the skis.

crud bad snow left after a disturbance.

crust a hard surface on the snow that sometimes supports a skier but not always.

depth hoar fragile crystals formed within the snow-pack.

drag a lift which pulls skiers uphill on their skis.

dynamic anticipation the winding-up of the body throughout a turn using all the rotary muscles in the torso.

dynamic stepping a way of initiating a turn.

edging angling the skis so that the metal edges bite into the snow.

fall-line the line a ball would take if rolling freely down a slope.

flow-line a curving line that results from a combination of momentum and gravity.

fracture line the line along which an avalanche breaks away.

Guide a qualified mountain guide who has a UIAGM carnet.

hard-pack hard, icy snow.

hypothermia lowering of the body's core temperature.

imaging see **visualising.**

italian hitch a knot used in belaying.

kick turn a way of turning on the spot.

kinaesthetic concerning the sensation of movement and motion.

off piste on an ungroomed slope.

open stance with feet the width of your hips apart.

piste prepared ski run or track.

ploughing skiing with the tips of the skis together and the tails apart, i.e. with the skis in a wedge shape.

powder light, dry snow.

real snow snow untouched by piste machines and other skiers; natural snow.

rime ice ice that forms on the windward side of objects, thereby indicating the direction of the wind.

safety strap a strap which attaches your ski to your ankle so that you do not lose it in the powder.

sastrugi features etched in the snow by wind.

schussing skiing straight down.

ski mountaineering see **touring.**

skins strips of synthetic material attached to the underside of skis which enable the skier to climb uphill.

slab section of a snow layer which has broken away.

snowploughing see **ploughing.**

stemming the action of moving the heel of a ski outwards.

telemarking a form of cross-country skiing which uses the telemark turn.

touring climbing and exploring mountains on skis using skins.

visualising mental rehearsal; used to prepare for, and thus enhance, performance.

wedge see **ploughing.**

whiteout the blending of snow-covered ground and sky when there is a mist, leaving no discernible horizon and therefore no fixed point of reference.

wind-slab snow deposited by the wind in a layer which does not adhere to other layers.

INDEX

Numbers in *italics* refer to illustrations.

FURTHER READING

General Skiing

Abraham, Horst. 1983. *Skiing Right.* Johnson Books, Colorado.
Bein, Vic. *Mountain Skiing.* The Mountaineers.
Ferguson, Sarah. 1989. *Skiing from the Inside.* Simon & Schuster, London.
Howe, John. 1983. *Skiing Mechanics.* Poudre, Colorado.
Hurn, Martyn. 1987. *Skiing Real Snow: The Handbook of Off-Piste Skiing.* Crowood Press, Ramsbury.
Hurn, Martyn. 1988. *Monoskiing.* Crowood Press, Ramsbury.
Joubert, Georges. 1978. *Skiing: an Art, a Technique.* Poudre, Colorado.
Loudis, Leonard, Lobitz, Charles and Singer. 1988. *Skiing out of your Mind.* Springfield Books, U.S.A.
Major, James and Larsson. 1979. *World Cup Ski Technique.* Poudre, Utah.
McCluggage, Denise. 1982. *The Centered Skier.* Bantam, New York.
Palmer, Stan. 1989. *Skiing Fit.* Crowood Press, Ramsbury.
Shedden, John. 1982. *Skilful Skiing.* E.P., Wakefield.
Shedden, John. 1986. *Skiing.* Crowood Press, Ramsbury.

Tejado-Flores, Lito. 1986. *Breakthrough on Skis.* Random House, New York.

Avalanches

Barton, Bob, and Wright, Blythe. 1985. *A Chance in a Million.* S.M.T.
Daffern, Tony. 1983. *Avalanche Safety for Skiers and Climbers.* Diadem.
Epp, Martin, and Lee, Stephen. 1987. *Avalanche Awareness.* The Wild Side, London.
Fraser, Colin. 1966. *Avalanches and Snow Safety.* John Murray.

Mountain Craft

Cliff, Peter. *Mountain Navigation.* D.E. Thompson.
Langmuir, E. *Mountain Craft and Leadership.* Cordee.
March, Bill. *Modern Rope Technique.* Cicerone Press.
March, Bill. *Modern Snow and Ice Techniques.* Cicerone Press.
Pedgley, David. *Mountain Weather.* Cicerone Press.
Wilkerson, T. 1985. *Medicine for Mountaineers.* The Mountaineers, Seattle.

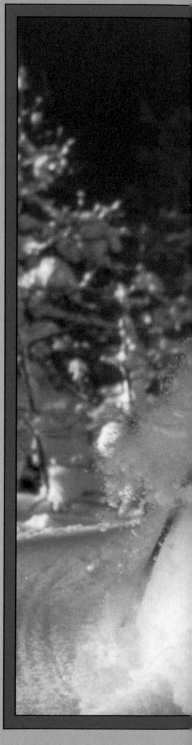

PHOTOGRAPHIC ACKNOWLEDGEMENTS

Allsport: Sylvie Chappaz 127; Giosanna Crivelli 56; Didier Givois front cover, 57 (top); F. St. Clair-Renard 57 (bottom)
Jeff Andrews 12 (top)
Breckenridge Ski Area Collection: Carl Scofield 111 (top left & right, bottom right), 115
Liz Cambell 112, 113 (top & bottom)
Sally Churcher 80 (top & bottom)
Copper Mountain Collection: 55, 106
Europa Sport: Dynastar Look Nordica 81 (top & bottom left); Mark Junak 73 (top); Mats Lindgren 15; Nordica 17 (top & bottom); Others 22, 78 (top left & right), 104, 105, 109
Fred Foxon 12 (bottom), 53 (top left & bottom left), 75
Alex Leaf 9, 68
John Mason 8 (bottom)
Ian McKenzie 110, 111 (bottom left)
Rupert Molloy 87 (bottom)
Planet Earth Pictures: Franz J. Camenzind 101 (top)
Premier Neige: Mark Junak 46, 77 (top & bottom), 114
Roger Rose 65 (top, middle & bottom), 72 (top, middle & bottom), 73 (bottom)
Lois Steenman-Clark 66 (top, middle & bottom), 67 (top left & right, bottom left), 78 (bottom), 79 (top, bottom left & right), 84 (top, middle & bottom right)